# SELF-PUBLISHING SECRETS

## by Gini Graham Scott, Ph.D.

### Author of 100+ Books
### 60 from Changemakers Publishing

**SELF-PUBLISHING SECRETS**

Copyright © 2017 by Gini Graham Scott

# TABLE OF CONTENTS

# INTRODUCTION

SELF-PUBLISHING SECRETS is based on a workshop series and talks I have conducted on self-publishing to several different groups in the San Francisco Bay Area. This is also being turned into a video.

It covers these main topics:
- The advantages of self-publishing a book
- How I can help you self-publish your book: my background in publishing
- Deciding on your overall purpose and goal
- Determining what to write about
- Creating an outline and timeline
- Getting your information
- Writing and editing your book
- Formatting your book for publication
- Publishing your book
- Creating a POD – Publishing on CreateSpace and other platforms
- Publishing an E-book – Publishing on Kindle and other platforms
- Creating an Audiobook – Publishing with ACX/Audible and other platforms
- Using a PDF to sell your book online
- Creating a course: using PowerPoints and videos
- Setting up your sequence for publishing
- Distributing and promoting your book
- Getting testimonials and reviews

# CHAPTER 1: WHY NOT FIND A TRADITIONAL PUBLISHER?

One of the first questions that comes up when I suggest self-publishing a book is "why." There are many reasons, but first I want to deal with the issue that comes up for many would-be authors – "I'd like to find a traditional publisher. Why can't I find a mainstream publisher?" Some writers even have visions of their book being a best seller. Why not approach a traditional publisher? Why self-publish?

First, let me start with a reality check.

If you are writing certain types of books, it is not likely that a traditional publisher, other than a very small one, will be interested, unless you have already developed a platform and have lots of followers. This largely applies to books in the self-help, popular business, relationships, and memoir categories, since these are very competitive genres. The major publishers want someone who is already very well-known. This means that you have about 50,000 or more followers and fans on Facebook or Twitter, have frequently appeared on the media, or have an active speaking program with 100+ audiences.

You might still find a traditional publisher for books in these regular genres, but this will probably be a small publisher with limited distribution; you will probably get little or no advance; and the publisher will do little or no PR for you. Basically, the major advantage of opting to go with a small publisher is they have a pre-established distribution network. But with little promotion, you will have limited sales and will get only a small royalty. Plus the publisher will have control, so you may be limited in your sales to other markets, including e-books, audiobooks, and international sales. You may also give up the possibility of dramatic and performance rights, should your book have potential as a documentary or feature film.

Then, too, if you sign with a publisher, you will generally face a long time before the book's release – generally a year to 18 months with the larger publishers, 6 to12 months with medium-sized publishers, and 3 to 4 months or longer with the smaller publishers. However, if the publisher has not paid you an advance, the publisher may feel under no compulsion to publish your book, and you may find after six months or a year, the publisher still has no plans to publish – which I experienced with a few publishers. Thus, while you may not lose any money, you may lose a lot of time and experience a lot of frustration.

Also, be aware that even if you do find an interested traditional publisher, the publisher will generally do little to promote the book. Commonly, with the exception of really big books with high profile authors, the publisher will send out a dozen or so books to major publications that do book reviews and to a few media and book reviewer contacts, but after that you are on your own. The publisher may be willing to send out book copies for you, if you find book reviewers who want a hard copy of your book to review or if you are interested in participating in a book festival or trade fair. But if there is any entry fee, typically you have to pay; the publisher doesn't normally do this.

If it's an academic book where interest is largely limited to a niche audience in your field, a trade publisher will probably not be interested unless you are a well-known authority. But if the reputation or prestige value is most important to you, do contact academic publishers first, since being published by an established press will contribute to your academic career, whereas a self-published book will have less authority in your field. If you don't find an academic publisher, you can always self-publish.

Similarly, if you have written a novel or a timely book on a topic that could have wide appeal, it can be worth it to pitch the book to editors and agents first and go the traditional route if there is interest. If not, you can self-publish.

Still another alternative is the hybrid model, where you pay a traditional publisher to publish your book, usually under a special imprint. For example, Wiley, a business book publisher; Hay House, a self-help, inspirational publisher; and Simon and Schuster, a general interest publisher, have set up divisions to publish books from authors who pay for their help with editing, design, marketing, and distribution. On the plus side, these publishers normally exercise some selectivity to be sure the book fits with their line and is a well-written book. This hybrid model can also be a good approach if you already have a built-in market, such as if you are speaking nationally on a particular topic or have an online marketing company, where you can expect several thousand customers. However, a disadvantage of this approach is that you have to pay a substantial amount through an upfront payment or an agreement to purchase a large number of books – generally about 20,000-30,000 copies. So if you don't have the customers or funds to commit to this method of publishing, a hybrid solution with a traditional publisher might not be the most realistic approach.

Thus, under most circumstances, it's better not to choose the traditional publishing route, since your book may not be likely to find a traditional publisher. Also, it may take too long for your book to be published if you want a book out quickly, because you are doing talks, workshops, or seminars, and would like your book to be available for sale and to show your authority in the field.

But there is an alternative to consider if your ultimate goal is a traditional publisher. Start with a short part of the larger book – perhaps 7000-10,000 words of a 60,000-80,000 word book, and publish that. You can use this short book to help build your platform. Then, perhaps a year or two later, submit a proposal to an established publisher for the larger book. Include your already completed chapters and describe the platform you have built up due to the growing number of attendees at your programs and your media appearances.

# CHAPTER 2: WHY SELF-PUBLISH A BOOK

Admit it. If you are reading this book, you are probably already considering self-publishing a book – or at least deciding between going the traditional route and self-publishing. So if you haven't already decided, or are trying to convince a spouse, family member, friend, business associate, or client to self-publish, let me count the many reasons for you.

- You have a message to share with others. This might be a book to support a cause or a creative project, like a novel, to express yourself and get recognition from others. Or perhaps you or someone you know have experienced a tragedy or been a victim of a terrible experience, and the book is a way of making sense of it, feeling better, or sharing what you have learned with others.

- You want to build your personal brand or your business. Generally, these will be short promotional books about you and your company or tips on how prospective clients or customers can help themselves, so they will hire you. Your book will help to show that you have the expertise to do these tasks more quickly and more effectively than they can themselves. Here I will be focusing on publishing this type of book.

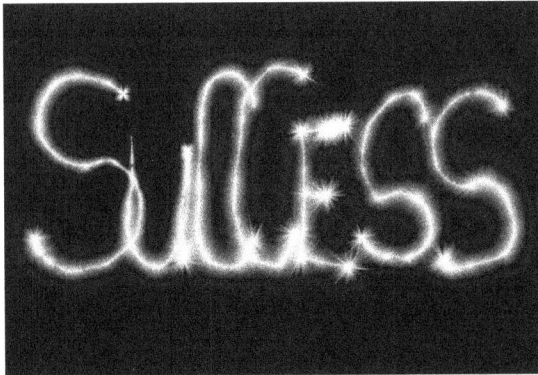

So what are the major reasons for self-publishing a book to build your brand or business? Let me count the whys.

## More Credibility and Visibility as You Show Off Your Knowledge

Among other things, you gain more credibility and visibility when you have a book. It's an ideal way to highlight what you do, provide some background on your company and yourself, or give a prospective client or customer some useful tips related to your business, which show you as the authority on the subject. You can include photos to show off the work you do, which is especially good for photographers, designers, architects, builders, and others with very visual work. But even those who work in an office can show off their meetings with clients, such as lawyers and financial planners.

## Quickly and Easily Get Out Your Message

Once you have written and edited your book, your book can be published in a matter of days, unlike the many months for publishing with a traditional publisher. And a few days after publication, you can have copies to use for displays or promotional hand-outs, as well as to sell books.

Your book can also be quick to write yourself or with the help of a ghostwriter, if it's one of these small books that are about 40 or 50 pages in length. These mini-books are becoming more and more popular, because they are fast to read – perhaps an hour or two, which is what people like today. You can easily publish them, including for free, if you can write and edit your book yourself. Or you can publish it for very little money, if you only need some help getting your book formatted and ready to publish.

## Make Your Book Available in Multiple Formats

Once you publish your book, you can sell it in multiple formats to multiple markets. You can sell your book as a PDF from your website or in the marketplaces for digital products, such as ClickBank. You can sell your book in print on Amazon, as an e-book on Kindle, and as an audiobook on Audible. You can also put your message into a PowerPoint and turn that into a video, or you can create a video with you as the spokesperson for your book and use that for promotion. Or announce your book on the social media or your website.

In short, there are numerous ways to publish, sell, and promote your book. And you can make money through book sales or through using your book to promote other services and products with the added clout a book offers.

## Build Your Brand

You can build your brand with your book or a book series, where each one features a different aspect of your business. For further brand identity, you can link the books in the series together with your logo or a photo of your company on the book jacket. For instance, feature your logo prominently on the front or back of the book, or perhaps have a photo of your company on the front cover, so each book is related to the other books in the series.

## Make Money

You can make money by selling your books or by using them to increase the sales of your products or services. For example, if you are selling a print-version of your book through a platform like CreateSpace, you can mark your book up two to four times over the cost of the books to you. And even after the sales commission is deducted, you earn about two to three times the book's cost. To illustrate, you can sell a book that costs you $2.15 a copy for $10.00 (or $9.95 which is a popular price point). If you are getting a 70% royalty on the book, that's about $7 a book – or $4.85 in profit for each book sold.

You can also make money by selling direct, such as if you do a talk or workshop based on your book and sell books there. Or you might sell a book direct from your website or sell it as a PDF through a digital platform, where the customers download the book. Here your costs are almost nothing; just a small labor cost for the time it takes to email the PDF to the customer. Or you can use an automatic responder that will handle the delivery for you, and you pay just a small subscription each month – say $19 for an introductory monthly subscription. So if you sell 10 books, each sale costs you about $2 per book; therefore on a $10 book, you net about $8. If you sell 20 books, your cost is about $1 a book or $9 in profit for each sale.

## Gain Prestige as a Published Author

Besides building your visibility and credibility, you can add to your prestige, since you can say you are a published author. You can bring your books to networking events to show off. Or if you are a speaker or panelist at an event, you can be introduced as a published author in addition to any other work you do.

## Show Prospective Clients What You Do

Rather than just telling clients what you do or explaining the benefits of your products or services, you can show them. You can use photos to show your everyday operations, your products in use, or the different types of work you have done for your clients.

Many people put information with photos on their website, which is fine. A book is an alternate way to show what you do, and you can readily pull out a book at an event or give away a promotional copy to a client. Many people like looking at something physical, and they can readily look at your book when they don't have access to a website or prefer holding something in their hands, rather than clicking on images on a website.

## Provide Tips to Clients Who Are More Likely to Hire You

You can also give clients tips on how to do something in your field, which might inspire them to initiate a project based on your ideas. Then, they may want to hire you as the expert to consult with them or do the work for them. Your tips can help them think about doing something they hadn't thought of doing before. And if they go ahead with a project, they may be more likely to hire you to help them, rather than looking for someone else to assist them. After all, they got the idea from your book.

For example, I had one contractor client who created a self-published book, which gave people tips on remodeling their kitchen. After they read the book, they realized all the things they would have to do and hired him.

## Use Your Book to Get Speaking Engagements

You can use your book to get speaking engagements, since your book helps to show you are an expert on that subject. As a result, it is easier to pitch yourself as a speaker or panelist to someone in an organization who organizes the programs. Or someone who reads your book may call you about speaking or being on a panel.

Once you have that speaking gig, you can use it to get clients. For example, I've been going to classes and conferences for speakers recently, and one approach many speakers recommend is giving a talk for 10 to 30 minutes, however much time the program organizers give you. Then, you use that time to give people information of value, such as how to do something, like how to beautify your home with tips from an interior designer. Finally, you conclude the talk by inviting people who are interested to attend a free strategy session for about an hour, where you will talk more about what they want to do and how you can help them do it.

For instance, if you are promoting a line of nutrition and diet products, your talk might be on several ways to get healthier. Later, when you meet individually with attendees who want to know more, you can go into more detail on what they can do and how your products can help them. Or if you are selling financial services, your talk might be about different investment programs. When you meet with the interested attendees, you can give them advice on what programs would be ideal for them and how you can set up an investment program based on what they need and want.

When you give one of these talks, bring flyers to distribute, which feature the different things you offer. But instead of featuring individual products or services with individual prices for products or hourly rates for services, create a package that provides value as a result of using your products or services. For instance, if you are pitching nutritional products, you might offer a series of products to take each month to improve one's health; if you are a financial coach, you might offer a package to help clients achieve some financial objective. That's the approach I have used in creating a package of going from an idea to a published book.

You also want to provide an attractive offer for buying your whole package now, such as providing a 20% to 30% discount when customers buy these products or services together, although you still offer an opportunity to purchase individual products or services on a per item or per hour basis if customers prefer that.

In short, whatever your product or service, you have a talk related to that which provides value. At the end of your talk, you offer to meet with people interested in learning more for about an hour. Then, in that strategy session, you spend about 20 to30 minutes giving prospective customers or clients tips and value in helping them know what to do. Then, you go into an enrollment process where you have a package of products and services, and you seek to enroll prospects in your package or invite them to buy individual products or services.

# CHAPTER 3: HOW I CAN HELP YOU CREATE YOUR BOOK: MY BACKGROUND IN PUBLISHING

Right now you may be asking, who am I to tell you why and how you need to self-publish. So let me tell you a little about myself.

I've published over a hundred books at this point. Fifty of these books were with the traditional publishers. Some books were published by the biggest publishers, including Random House, Simon & Schuster, Contemporary Books, Warners, Rowman & Littlefield, AMACOM, ABC-Clio, New Harbinger, Avon Books, Sourcebooks, Nolo Press, and more. Some of these books included: *Mind Power: Picture Your Way to Success in Business; Want It, See It, Get It!, Resolving Conflict; The Truth About Lying; A Survival Guide for Working with Humans...Bad Bosses...and Employees;* and more. I've had several dozen books licensed in foreign markets. A few of these books are still selling after 30 years.

I started self-publishing through Changemakers Publishing. These books have been on a number of topics, including self-help, popular business, marketing and sales, memoirs, social trends, and creativity. I even published some kids' books.

I got into self-publishing about ten years ago when I was a member of ASJA, the American Society for Journalists and Authors. At the time, iUniverse was one of the first self-publishing companies, and it had a program with ASJA, whereby iUniverse would take any previously published book that was no longer in print and put it back into print at no charge on the ASJA imprint. So I had about two dozen books published that way with a non-exclusive agreement. I just had to send iUniverse two copies of my published book, and they would do the rest. In fact, I still get royalties on some of these books.

Then, CreateSpace, an online self-publishing platform, came along, offering a simple way to publish your own print-on-demand books using a Word document or a PDF, and uploading this onto one of its template designs. The company was formerly called BookSurge, and it became CreateSpace after Amazon took it over. The advantage of this platform is it offered a way to publish books for free using its templates. After you created a master file with your text and graphics, you could order as many or as few books as you wanted, and the book would be made available for sale on Amazon – and later on Kindle.

At first I just republished books that were already on iUniverse, since I had a non-exclusive arrangement with them, meaning that I could publish my books anywhere. I started with my books on visualization, improving work relations, conflict resolution, and lying. Then, I began doing originals, such as a kid's book, some books of photos of graffiti I took by the beach in San Francisco, and a workbook on working with people with disabilities.

Now I mostly do original books on all sorts of topics – both books of my own and for clients. Typically, these are 50 to 70 pages, though some have been as little as 30 or 40 pages, and few have been as long as 300 pages or more. I also started publishing a series of books with photos and graphics, such as two books with quotes on anger and gratitude, a kid's picture book about a meerkat who had trouble standing up, and a series of books on using emails successfully to build your business.

Here are some examples of my self-published books.

I have a number of books on how to become a writer or how to work with a writer or ghostwriter, how to find publishers and agents, and how to deal with contracts. Some examples here include: *How to Find Publishers and Agents and Get Published; How to Get Published and Deal with Clients, Co-Writing, Copyrights, and Contracts;* and *How to Find and Work with a Good Ghostwriter.*

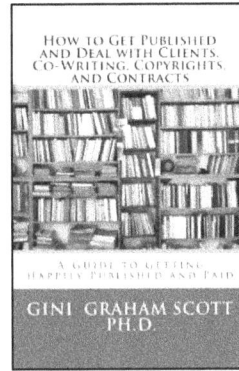

Some examples of self-help books that I've done are *Mind Power* and *The Empowered Mind*, which deal with visualization, and *30 Days to a More Powerful Memory*. I don't have a particularly good memory, but my publisher came to me and said "We'd like to have a book on memory," so I wrote it and it really helped me improve my memory for a while. Some other self-help books are *Get That Innovative Edge, Affirming Your Success,* and *The Anger Book*.

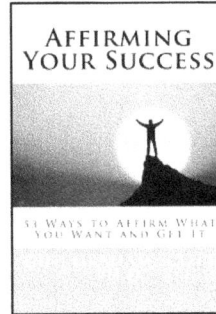

I wrote the last two titles by collecting quotes, which are very easy to get on the Internet. You just do a Google search for "quotes" and the subject you want the quotes to be about, and you'll see hundreds of them. I'm doing another book on gratitude, where I've gotten several hundred quotes, and I'm combining them with pictures and my comments on the topic.

As for popular business books, I've done everything from *Success in MLM* and having sales parties to improving relationships in the workplace. Some of these titles are *Success in MLM, Network Marketing, and Personal Selling; Let's Have a Sales Party; Work with Me;* and *The Truth about Lying.* I also did a series of eight books called *The Complete Guide to Email Marketing* and a workbook on *Working with People with Disabilities.*

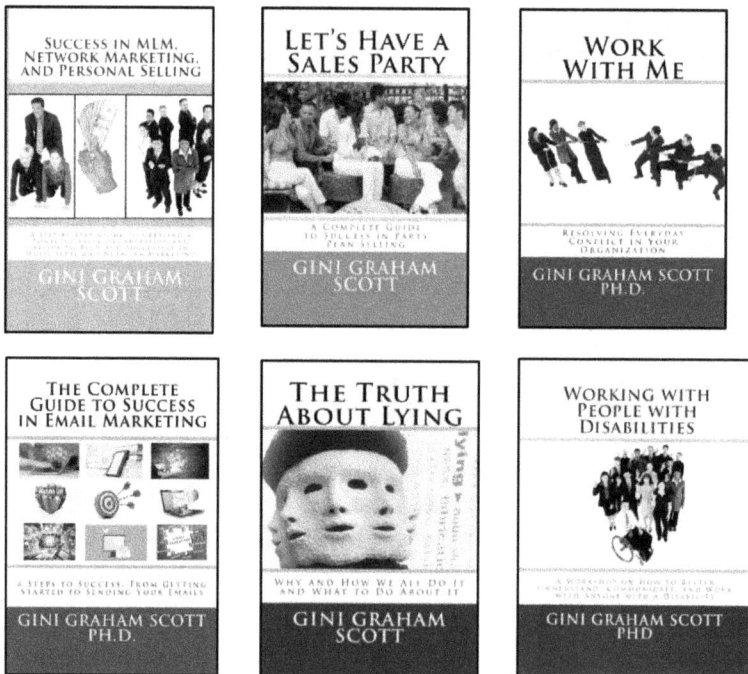

All these books have the same kind of look, since I chose one of these templates for almost all my books, and CreateSpace's templates makes it really easy. You get a photograph and put that in the template, and you can modify the background color, theme, font, and other elements for a distinctive look, though you can create your own cover, too.

Also, I do ghostwriting, and I have published a lot of books for clients using the CreateSpace platform. Plus I have helped some of them find traditional publishers, when they have a book with broad appeal. The CreateSpace platform is free, and anyone can do it themselves with a completed Word document or PDF. But a lot of people need help in navigating through the platform and in preparing the additional copy needed for the cover and a book description. So some people hire me to guide them through the process, because they don't know what to do and find the platform confusing.

And here are some books that I've done for clients. One is a remodeling book for a client *Remodeling Stress.* He was initially planning to publish with a self-publishing company that was going to charge him $5.58 for each book, and I got the price down for him through CreateSpace to $2.15 a book. Another book for a client is *My Doom Loop,* a self-help book where the author came up with her own cover. She worked with a graphic designer who designed her cover using CreateSpace's specs based on the size of the book and the number of pages, though CreateSpace has 30 different templates you can choose from.

*The Deep Sea* uses another template that this client chose, and I did a series of books for a client on the criminal justice system, starting with *The Price of Justice in America*. He has written a half-dozen books so far on criminal justice in America, and I have been doing a PR campaign for him working with a publicist. He's doing speaking engagements now, and I'm helping him create a video series where he puts the highlights from each of his books into a PowerPoint presentation, does a voice-over, and we turn that into a video. After that, we'll use the videos to set up a course on the subject, which we'll do through ClickBank, a sales platform for digital products, including courses and PDFs.

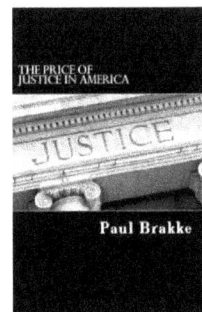

So that's an overview of what I've done in publishing. You can see more information about me on my websites www.ginigrahamscott.com and www.changemakerspublishingandwriting.com. And if you put my name in Google, you'll get about 43,000 hits.

# CHAPTER 4: THE TEN MAJOR STEPS TO A SELF-PUBLISHED BOOK

Following is an overview of the 10 major steps to a published book. Then, I'll go through each one in more detail.

The first step is to decide <u>your overall purpose and goal</u>, which is why you are writing the book and who are you writing this for.

Step #2 is to decide <u>what you want to write about</u>. Sometimes people aren't sure, when they are in a number of different fields, so they don't know what to do. They want to use a book to build their brand, but they're not sure what their brand is going to be. So they might ultimately want to write two books, or they may decide which to prioritize first. Part of my initial discussion with somebody is to clarify their topic, if they're not sure what to write about.

Step #3 is <u>creating an outline and timeline</u> for what you plan to write about. You determine what information you need to get and how long it will take you to get it.

Step #4 is <u>getting your information</u>. Think about what you already have and where you need to get the additional information. Is this information in notes? Do you need to do interviews? Can you talk into a recorder or your phone to describe the planned chapters?

In some cases, to help people develop their book, I'll do interviews with them to help them find their information. Sometimes people who want to write a book are not really writers, or what they have written is badly written, so it needs to be re-worked.  There are several ways to do this -- people can talk into a tape recorder; I or someone else can interview them; they might do a workshop or seminar and record that.

Once you have a recording, you can get a transcript, since it's best to work from that because we talk much faster than we write.  So a transcript is the only way to get all the details from a talk.

If you don't already have someone to produce your transcript, you can quickly get a recording transcribed through a transcript service, such as rev.com, which charges $1 a page. Within four or five hours, you get your complete transcript back.  The company has a whole team of people doing these transcripts.

Step #5 is writing your book.  Divide it up in chapters and devote several hours a day for a few weeks until this is done.

Finally, you have to edit and polish up your writing or hire an editor or ghostwriter to write your book for you.  Some people may experience some resistance at this stage for various reasons.  Some people take a very long time to write their manuscript if they are very busy or not really writers.  Some may be held back by feeling their book has to be perfect, though a good way to get through this block is to divide the writing into two stages.  In the first stage, the creative phase, you just write whatever you want for each chapter.  Or divide the chapters into sections and write each of these quickly.  In the second analytic phase, you return to the manuscript and edit, revise, and move things around.

The amount of time people take for writing varies. Professional writer typically write much more quickly. For example, I usually write about 10-15 pages a day, or about 3000-4500 words, averaging about 1000 words an hour. Based on that, I can usually complete a short book of about 10,000-15,000 words in about a week, which is a common length for a self-published book.

Step #6 is formatting your book for publication.  This is where you set up your book in the type of file required for publication, such as a Word document, or a PDF.  You have to set up the page size and format, too.  If you use the most common 6"x9" format, set up your manuscript with that page size and set the margins depending on the number of pages in your book.  For a short book, figure on about .75 margins on the left or right and between .75 and 1" for the top and bottom margins.   Also, if necessary, reset the line spacing, get rid of extra paragraphs, add in headers, and update your table of contents to reflect the new pages.

Step #7 is publishing your book, following the guidelines for the platform you are using.  For instance, with CreateSpace the publication process involves uploading a properly formatted file and completing the steps for the cover template, or you upload a final PDF which follows Createspace's specs for creating the back and front cover and spine.

For Step #8, you expand your book's reach by creating your book in other formats. The most well-known other format is publishing an e-book on Kindle. You can also create an e-book for Smashwords, which distributes your e-book on a dozen other platforms. You can additionally distribute a PDF through your website, ClickBank, and other digital stores.

Another format that many people don't realize that they can easily set up is an audio book sold through Audible, as long as it meets certain technical requirements. Anyone can do a recording, though you have to meet very exacting standards for a professional audio recording. But ACX is a great format for finding a professional narrator to record your book. Then, you either share the royalty or you offer the narrator a fixed payment for recording the book. Generally, it takes about two hours of recording time for every hour of audio, since you have to edit and clean up the original audio. Ideally, find a highly skilled narrator. A narrator will speak about 9300 words an hour and charge about $200 per finished hour. So figure on about $200 for every 10,000 words in your manuscript.

Step #9 involves distributing and promoting your book. The distribution part can be relatively easy, especially if you publish your book through CreateSpace or Kindle. Your book is immediately made available through Amazon, which handles about 70% of book sales and has expanded distribution to libraries, chains, and other countries. What is more difficult is promoting your book, since you have to actively promote it in various ways, from using the traditional and social media to setting up events, participating in book fairs and trade shows, and doing workshops and seminars.

Finally, Step #10 is getting testimonials and reviews, which will help you gain credibility and visibility and support your efforts to distribute and promote your book. Generally, you have to be proactive to get these testimonials and reviews by reaching out to publishers and reviewers interested in books on your subject. If they are interested, send them each a PDF or hard copy and hope that they write good things about your book, so you can use that review in your PR.

In the next chapters, I'll talk about these ten key steps to self-publishing in more depth.

# CHAPTER 5: DECIDING ON YOUR OVERALL PURPOSE AND GOAL

For the first step – deciding on your overall purpose and goal – ask yourself, "Why do I want to write this book?" and "What do I want to say?" Keep your answer short, to a sentence. Also ask "Who is my primary market or markets?" and consider how important it is to write your book now. If there are other priorities to do first, restate the question to ask "How important is it for me to write my book after I finish some current commitments and priorities?"

Then, consider your book's major type or genre, since you want to position your book to fall into one of the popular categories. That designation will help you market, distribute, and promote the book, since you can target your sales and promotion campaign to that target market.

You also need to limit this market, so you can zero in on it. As they say, if you say your book is for "anybody," "anyone," or "everybody," you are targeting nobody, which is usually a losing market proposition. Therefore, it's best to start with a particular niche and determine the characteristics of that market, so you can target your marketing to that segment. Then, you can expand from that niche to other markets, as you are successful in your initial niche.

The major niches for books today include the following. If your book overlaps categories, such as a book which might be considered either a work or career book or a self-help book, decide on which market to emphasize and promote it to that audience first.

These major niches are:

- a self-help, personal development, or inspirational book
- a popular business book,
- a how-to book, such as a book on crafts or how to fish,
- a memoir or family legacy book,
- a general interest book on social trends or topics in the news.

Once you identify your primary market for what you want to say, that will shape your approach to your subject, including the voice or tone of your writing, the photo for your cover, and more. Consider the benefits that market will get from your book and highlight those.

For example, I recently wrote a number of memoirs for a family member or spouse who was writing the book because their partner or parent was dying. So they wanted what their loved one remembered put into a book, before it was lost forever, due to that person dying or losing his memory. In some cases, an elderly person may want to leave the book as a legacy to their family when they are gone, and rather than a video, which can only touch the surface of their life, they want a more in-depth bio to leave to their children or other family members. Usually, there is some urgency to completing these memoirs quickly, even within a few months, in order to capture the thoughts or memories of the subject of the book before their recollections are gone.

Also consider the lengthy of the book. If you're trying to find a traditional publisher, the book should be about 250-300 pages or about 60,000-90,000 words. But if you are self-publishing, a lot of people are writing and publishing very short books that are between about 35 to 50 pages, up to 60 to 70 pages. The minimum is 24 pages to publish your book with CreateSpace, though with large type and photos or illustrations, that's an easy minimum to meet.

Also think about what makes your book unique and different. In some fields, everybody is talking about the same kind of thing, such as in self-help, inspirational or popular business books. So think of some way in which your book will be different. You want a message that will help you stand out, such as a different theme or metaphor for a self-help or inspirational book, or a different method to achieve success in a business book. An example might be using stories about pets to illustrate ways to achieve satisfaction and happiness in life for a self-help book, or fishing techniques to illustrate setting and fulfilling achievement goals for a business book. Just check what other books on your topic are out there to be sure that no one has used such parallels and examples in another book.

# CHAPTER 6: WHAT TO WRITE ABOUT

Once you know the overall purpose or goal of your book, decide what to include in your book. Some of the major sources of material to include are:
- your personal experiences or observations,
- content from your workshops or seminars,
- research on your industry,
- others' accounts about the industry.

## Your Personal Experiences or Observations

Your experiences or observations are central in a memoir or narrative, and they can be an ideal way to illustrate the points you are making in a self-help or business book. Some writers start off with a personal example at the beginning of a chapter, or you can weave in your story with a discussion of what you have learned from the experience to provide insights to others.

For example, one writer described his harrowing experiences attending elite schools in Nazi Germany when he was a boy, and he discussed how he learned the importance of staying silent and following the rules, even as he quietly broke them with those he trusted. Later, he applied that approach when he was studying in the United States to become a research scientist, since he had to remain silent about certain things, while talking about other experiences to advance his career.

## Content from Your Workshops or Seminars

If you are doing workshops or seminars, you can use this information for your book in two ways:
- If you are preparing material for your program, you can save this and revise it to fit into your book.
- You can record your program on a recording device, such as a Zoom recorder, or on your smartphone. Then, have the recording transcribed, using a transcriber or send it off to a transcribing service like www.rev.com, which also has an app you can download onto your phone. You can click record on your phone, and after you are finished, immediately send it to the transcribing service, or you can email the file to the service's website. The cost is $1 a page, and you can get the transcript back within 24 hours or even sooner. I typically get my recordings back in 4 to 5 hours.

It is important to revise any audio material from your workshop, seminar, or live recording, since we talk very differently from our writing. Our speaking style is more informal, and often you may add in digressions as you think of different examples, stories, or information in the news.

## Research on Your Industry

Examples of what others are doing in your industry can be a great way to supplement your own experience. These accounts can add to your credibility and authority by showing that you are knowledgeable of what others in your field are doing, so you can speak more authoritatively about the latest developments and show that you are up on the latest in your industry.

It is easy to look for this information on the Internet. Just put key words in Google Search and see what articles turn up. Print out those that are relevant. Use a few related word searches to be sure you cover your topic. As you find useful information, credit the source with a footnote or end note, and add it to the bibliography.

So you don't bog down the reader with extensive footnotes, since this is not an academic project, put them in a reference section at the end of each chapter or in end notes in the back of the book. Or if you prefer, include a reference section at the end of your book with all of the references, and skip the footnotes, or endnotes.

The usual convention in the bibliography is to put the last name first and then the first name and any middle name or initial, followed by the article title and publication or the book title and publisher, followed by the date. In the footnoted or endnotes, the formatting is much the same as the bibliography, except that the author's name is written with the first name first, followed by any middle name or initial and last name.  For more details, use a style book.  The three main conventions are Chicago Style, MLA, and APA style.  Use the one you prefer.

If the research involves finding a few articles or other references, you can easily do this yourself in an hour or two.  But if you plan extensive research, consider hiring an assistant. You can readily find one by putting an announcement in any neighborhood online forum you belong to, or on Craigslist for your city. For a lot of research, I use assistants who do the searching and print out the articles they find.  Otherwise if the search is going to take about an hour, I do the research myself.

## Others' Accounts about the Industry

You can look at other accounts about the industry, if someone has an online course or is offering a PDF on your subject.  You will often find such offerings on Facebook, and once you click to show an interest in a class or PDF, the advertiser will typically ask for your email and will send you additional information there.  Another source of information about your industry is ClickBank and other digital marketing platforms, which feature classes and PDFs on different subjects.

## Use a Combination of Sources

Finally, whatever your topic, you can combine different sources of information together.  In fact, using multiple sources is a good idea, since it combines your own experiences with other sources that help to support what are saying.

# CHAPTER 7: CREATING AN OUTLINE AND TIMELINE

Your outline is important for shaping the material you collect into an organized series of chapters. Or, alternatively, you can create your outline after you have your overall purpose and goal to guide your collection of information. Then, too, your outline can evolve as you gather information and decide that there are additional topics to cover or topics you no longer want to include in your book.

Thus, consider your outline and timeline an evolving document, though it's good to initially create an outline and timeline to structure your plan for your book. This plan should indicate what you want to include and create a schedule of what to do and when to complete the book, though both the outline and timeline can change along the way.

Your outline can also help you in laying out the future chapters. And if you are seeking a traditional publisher, you can use your outline to write a book proposal, which includes an overview, chapter by chapter outline, and section on the appeal of the book. The outline will additionally guide you in doing a search for competing books in your field for the competitive marketing section, and you can use the outline to help you decide which one, two, or three chapters to include as sample chapters in the proposal.

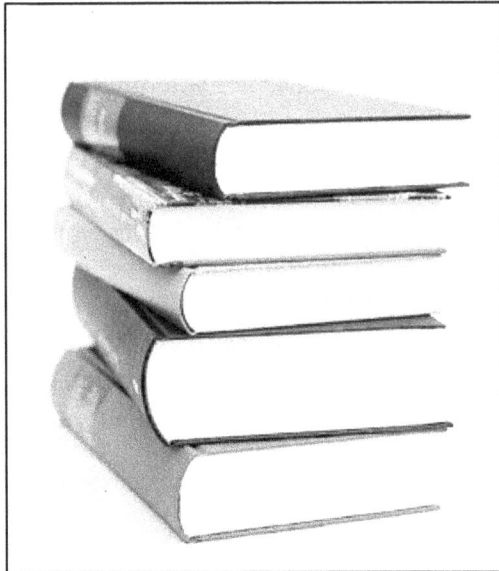

The main considerations to think about in creating your outline and timeline are these:

- Selecting an overall theme and focus,
- Choosing a working title,
- Deciding on your overall tone or style,
- Organizing the book into chapters,
- Assessing the time needed to get the information together,
- Determining the time needed for writing and editing each chapter,
- Creating a schedule and estimating the time to complete your book

I'll briefly describe each of these sections in more detail.

## Selecting an Overall Theme and Focus

You probably already have determined your overall theme and focus in selecting your purpose and goal. But if your information gathering and research has been devoted to finding out what you want to do, now is the time to decide on the main focus or theme of your book. Use the insights you have gained to clearly outline your plan for creating the book.

## Choosing a Working Title

If you are seeking a traditional publisher, the publisher will normally choose the final title, but in self-publishing, you decide. Start with a working title, and you can always change it before you publish.

In choosing your title, research other titles that have already been published, so you don't pick the same title or one that is very similar to another title. If you want a general title to refer to a whole field, such as self-hypnosis, the Paleolithic diet, or acupuncture, use that word in the title, but add a few other distinguishing words, such as "The Secrets of...," "The Complete Guide to..." or "How You Can Gain Success with..."

It's best to choose a title where you use the keywords someone will use to search for information on a topic, rather than trying for something clever or writing a title that sounds like sales hype, such as: "A Breakthrough Underwater Diet Discovery" for a book about using algae in a new diet program.

Consider trying out your title on business associates to see which has the most resonance. Then, pick the one that people seem to understand and like the most.

## Deciding On Your Overall Tone or Style

Before you start writing, decide on your style and voice for the book. If you are working with a writer or ghostwriter, give that person suggestions or even a sample you have written or spoken to show the style you like.

A key consideration is whether you want a more conversational or folksy tone or a more serious, authoritative one. Your style should also be related to the subject and how you approach it, if you give any talks, workshops, or seminars.

For example, if you are writing about your journey in recovering from an illness or personal tragedy, you may want a more intimate conversational style, where you talk to each individual reader. On the other hand, if you are reporting on recent trends in health care and how readers can plan for their health needs, a more authoritative tone might be more suitable.

## Organizing Your Book into Chapters

Now organize the planned contents for your book into chapters. One approach is to list and describe the main topics of your book in the overview, and turn each one of these topics into chapters. Or use your introduction to describe the purpose of your book, what topics you will cover, how you came to write the book, and a little about yourself. Then, quickly mention the major topics you will cover, and turn the topics and subtopics into chapters.

Alternatively, if you prefer writing your book with a more organic approach, such as if you are writing an autobiography in chronological order, you can write out much or all of the book, using a stream of consciousness. You can then organize your book into chapters and write the overview last, though this approach is less usual.

In any case, once you have divided your book into chapters, aim for 10-25 pages per chapter. Later, as you write, if you find a chapter is much shorter, consider combining it into a previous or subsequent chapter. If a chapter runs longer – say 35 pages or more, consider dividing that chapter into one or two smaller chapters. In making this division, look for natural break points in the subject and put those into separate chapters. Should you have several chapters that might be grouped together, you might divide your book into two or three parts, and call them Part I, Part II, and Part III, and title each part accordingly. You can reference the way you have divided up the book in the overview.

For example, say you are writing a book about how to get a good deal on a real estate property. "Part I: Understanding the Real Estate Market" might provide an overview of trends in the real estate market and what to look for in selecting a property. "Part II: Finding a Property" might cover how to look for properties, with or without a real estate agent, and how to further investigate those properties you are interested in. And "Part III: Negotiating and Closing the Deal" might describe how to negotiate to get the most favorable terms, when to walk away from a bad deal, and how to make an offer and write up the paperwork for the sale.

However you gather the information you need, once you decide on your chapters, it's a good idea to create folders for each one. I like to use physical folders, but if all your information is in digital form, you can create folders for each topic within a folder for your book. Or have both physical and digital files. In this case, you have any digital files in the book folder on your computer, but you also print out the documents and put the printouts for each item in the corresponding folder. I like the physical folders, because this enables me to mark on each printout what information I want to use, and I can easily move documents around and put them in any order. If I try to do this online, it takes me much longer to move files, and I can easily forget what's where, whereas when I see everything in front of me, I can quickly note what that article is about and what I have marked that I want to use with underlines or brackets.

Once you have organized your material by folders, with your information on a different topic in different folders, you can use that information to write one chapter at a time from that information. But you are never locked into that organization. Later, if you want, you can reorganize how you present your information by moving a topic from one chapter to another as appropriate.

## Assessing the Time to Obtain Information

Now that you know what you are writing, have gotten the information you need or are still doing research, consider how much time it will take you or a writer or researcher you are working with to obtain any additional information.

In some cases, you may have already assembled this information. In other cases, you may have some of it, know what you still need, and plan to obtain it. Whatever your process, make a rough estimate of the time you need for getting the necessary material, so you can factor that in to the time required to write and edit your book.

To illustrate, when I am writing a book based on interviews, I determine how many hours are likely to be needed for interviewing, reviewing transcripts, and research. Say I am doing 6 hours of interviews. I know each hour of the interview will turn into a transcript of about 15 pages or 90 pages for all the interviews, and it will take me about an hour to review the transcript and mark what I want to include in a write up. Then, if I'm doing the research, I'll figure on another 1 to 2 hours to look for and print out the relevant articles. Or if extensive research is required, I'll bring in an assistant and estimate how many hours that person will need to do the job.

## Determining the Time for Writing and Editing Each Chapter

Next consider how much time you need for writing, after you have the needed information from interviews, research, transcripts of recordings, and other sources. To estimate the time, project the total number of words or pages and estimate how long it will take to write and later edit all of the pages. Base this estimate on your typical time for writing and editing.

For example, if I am writing a chapter with 15 pages, that's about 4500 words, based on my writing 300 words per page. Since I write about 1200 words an hour, that would be about 4 hours to write, plus another 2 hours to edit, since I edit what I have written at about 5 or 6 pages an hour. So probably I would complete that 15 page chapter in 2 days, since I like to write on one project for about 3 hours a day.

## Creating a Schedule and Estimating the Time to Complete Your Book

Finally, estimate the time to completely write and edit the book. To do so, combine the number of hours for writing and editing each chapter to determine the total time you need. Also, figure on how many days you need for all of the chapters, based on whether you can write and edit your book on consecutive days, or whether you need to fit your writing time into your schedule for work and personal activities.

For example, as noted above, I know I can write about 3 pages with about 300 words on a page or about 1200 words an hour. Thus, if I'm writing a book of about 10,000 words, I can figure it will take about 8 1/2 hours to write it, and since I usually write for about 3 to 4 hours a day on one project, it will take me about 2 to 3 days to write this book. Then, since I typically edit about 5 or 6 pages an hour when I have written something, I figure on another 3 or 4 hours or another day for editing. I usually do this writing or editing over several consecutive days during the week, unless I have to skip a day due to meetings.

Whatever your situation, block out the time when you can work on your book. Then, estimate how much time over how many days it is likely to take you to write the whole book. If you find you are writing and editing more quickly or more slowly, modify your schedule accordingly as you go along. If a sudden emergency occurs, factor that in to your time schedule, too.

# CHAPTER 8: GETTING YOUR INFORMATION

You can get your information for your book from numerous sources, some already mentioned. To summarize, your sources can include the following:

- <u>Notes and journals</u>. You can write up your thoughts and observations on a regular basis, preferably each day. Put them on your phone or laptop, computer, or keep a handwritten journal. Then, organize this material by the topic or chapter, or for a memoir, use your notes to create a chronological record.

- <u>Recording yourself</u>. You can easily record yourself by talking into your smart phone or a special recorder, like a Zoom recorder. Another option is to create a recording on a teleseminar or webinar platform, or through a radio platform like Blogtalk radio. You can also record yourself doing a video on Periscope or Facebook Live, and use the audio. Whether you have an audience or not, talk as if someone is there. Then, get a transcript of your talk and revise that into copy for your book.

When you arrange to record yourself, it is helpful to start with an outline where you indicate the main topics you plan to talk about. This will you keep on topic, and you will have less revising and editing to do to turn your transcript into a book.

- <u>Recording your workshops or seminars</u>. If you are doing a workshop or seminar, record that. All you need is an audio recording, or if you have your program videotaped, pull the audio track from that. Then, turn the audio into a transcript. Let those at the workshop know you are recording it, though assure people that anything they say about themselves will be confidential, since you can edit out whatever they say if they don't want to be recorded. Though I haven't found it necessary to use release forms, since I'm just writing up the content in the recordings and not using any names or personal information, you can give everyone a release form to sign. The form is to indicate that they are giving you permission to record them or want their personal information excluded from your book.

- Research on the Internet and buying books. Almost anything you want to find out is on the Internet somewhere, so you can search for it and download it or print it out. The only major exception to getting free information on the internet is that you may need to buy books on your topic. However, you may find PDF files of many books, especially older ones that are out of print, on a website where you can download or print the PDF.

When you plan to do a search in Google on your topic, make a list of the 5 or 6 most relevant terms. Then, conduct the search with those terms or with those terms in a common phrase. For example, if you are writing a book about making money by flipping houses, put in terms like "real estate sales," "housing sales," "flipping houses," and "real estate investing."

After getting results from your search, look for the most popular articles on the topic. These will normally be listed based on their key words and popularity. Generally, each page from this search will feature about 15 items, with 3 to 5 sponsored listings on many pages. Just look for articles on the 1$^{st}$ or 2$^{nd}$ page, which can include the three to five sponsored articles per page. Sometimes these articles will suggest other terms or phrases to search for, and if so, try searching with them.

To determine what books to get, put the phrases you are using for your Internet search and your book title in the Amazon search box and see what turns up. You might get up to 5 or 10 of the most popular books on the subject. As in a Google search, there are typically about 15 books listed.

Interviews with other people. In some cases, you want to interview other people for your book. Usually, you want to do these interviews with someone who is an expert on the topic of your book, though if they have written something, you can get the same or similar information from that. If the person has written material, use the interview to expand upon what the person has already said.

In other cases, you might want to interview people who have had an experience discussed in your book. For example, I wrote a series of books on workplace relationships that involved interviewing people about how they dealt with their boss or colleagues in different situations. For another book on ethical choices and conflicts, I interviewed two dozen people who had faced an ethical dilemma. For a book on lies by sociopaths, I interviewed people who had been the victim of a sociopathic liar and a few people who had told lies as a sociopath. I found these interview subjects through personal referrals, posting notices on an online neighborhood forum, and by making an announcement in a Facebook group and a LinkedIn group devoted to the subject.

Ideally, do these interviews in person, if the interviewee is in a nearby location, where you can go to the person's home or office or they can come to you. As another possibility, set up the interview on Skype, on the phone, or through a teleseminar or webinar service. Use your phone or recording device to record and get a transcript, as previously described.

Let the interviewee know how much time you need for the interview – 20 to 30 minutes is a good time to schedule for in advance, though sometimes an interview will go longer if the person is agreeable. Should the interviewee want a shorter time for the interview, say 10-15 minutes, adjust the questions you ask accordingly, so you get answers to your most important questions first.

To conduct the interview, it is helpful to create the list of questions to ask in advance and email them to the interviewee a few days – or at least one day – before the interview, so he or she is prepared. Review the questions before the interview and be prepared to ask follow-up questions suggested by the person's answers to your questions.

Working with a coach, interviewer or ghostwriter. If you don't have the time or interest in doing the research or conducting the interviews, you can hire a research assistant, interviewer, or ghostwriter to obtain this information for you. Commonly, if you are already working with a ghostwriter for your book, the ghostwriter can conduct the interviews and/or do the research for you, or you can have different people do the research, interviews, and writing.

As an example, besides being the ghostwriter for a book, I have done interviews and worked with a team of assistants to do Internet research for a number of clients. Most recently these clients have included a doctor writing a memoir about his experiences with end-of-life care, a professor doing a series of books on the criminal justice system, and a women helping her elderly husband write a memoir about his experiences growing up in Nazi Germany.

- Getting transcripts and editing the copy. Whenever you are working with an audio file, whether from a recording, workshop, or interviews, get a transcript. If you are doing the talking, it's difficult to also take notes, and when you are interviewing others, you can only get a small fraction of what they say. If you listen to a recording and take notes, it's slow going, and usually you can't take notes fast enough, so you have to repeatedly go back to get some detail you missed. So even if you are just looking for highlights from a recording for your book, it can make more sense to get a transcript. Then, select from it what to use.

For example, if you try to take notes from a 1 hour recording, it might take you about 3 hours; whereas it will cost about $60 at $1 a minute for a transcript, so it seems worth it to save you the time of doing it yourself.

When you get a transcript, you can't simply use it "as is" in your book. Most people use common fillers like "Ems," "Ahs," and "You knows" when they talk, and some transcribers will include these. Plus people go off on tangents, which don't fit well in a book. Or you may respond to a question, so you provide information before you planned to cover that topic according to your original order of chapters. As a result, you often have to reorganize the material in your transcript, so it goes in the appropriate chapter in your book.

# CHAPTER 9: WRITING YOUR BOOK

When it comes to writing your book, you can write it yourself, work with a consultant or coach to guide your through the process, or hire a ghostwriter to write your book. If you work with a ghostwriter, you can create a schedule for them or they can create a schedule for you and themselves.

## Writing the Book Yourself

If you write you book yourself, assuming you have outlined the book and organized it into chapters, I recommend dividing the writing process into two phases. In the first creative phase, write the first draft following the outline and quickly write whatever you want to say. If you want to quote someone else from your online research, from their book, or from an interview, similarly quickly write whatever you want to say. Include quote marks before and after their quote to indicate that you have what they have said or written verbatim.

Then, in the second analytical or critical phase, do the editing, where you eliminate any repetition, reorganize anything that should be moved somewhere else, and make any corrections for grammar and typos, and tighten up the language. In this editing process, you fine tune whatever you have to say and create your final copy, so the book is ready to go to the publisher.

In either phase, you can add any photos or illustrations by inserting the JPEGs in the copy, though after you finalize the copy, you may need to adjust the placement of photos that have been pushed off a page or out of alignment due to changes in the copy. Or you may find a better more suitable place for a photo.

For example, after I write the first draft in the creative phases, it's usually fairly well organized, since I have been working with a predetermined outline, although I often do this in my head rather than creating a written outline, since I have written many books for myself and others. But if this is your first book or you only have written a few books, I suggest starting with a written outline you can follow.

If you have a fairly simple editing job, requiring minimal copy corrections and no major reorganization, it can be faster to edit the manuscript on the computer. However, if extensive editing is required, it is better to print out the draft of the manuscript, which is what I do.

Once you print out the manuscript, you can read it like a reader would normally read a book, so you can read more carefully than if you were just editing on the computer. That's because you are better able to see more detail and look at the manuscript as a whole, rather seeing just a page or parts of pages on a screen. Seeing the manuscript printed out also enables you to better move things around, using arrows and letters to indicate what gets moved where. Otherwise, when you see pages or parts of pages on a screen, it can be hard to remember what gets moved where, or you can easily move something to the wrong place.

For example, when I do this kind of editing, I will write down an "A" or "B" to indicate the paragraphs to be moved and an "A" or "B" in the place where I want to move that section. Sometimes I use arrows to indicate what gets moved with a left pointing arrow and designate where it gets moved with a right pointing arrow. Then, I use these markings as a guide when I move a block of copy or sentence on my computer. By contrast, if I was only doing the editing on my computer, after I make a couple of changes, I usually forget what goes where. It may take a little longer to do this two-step editing process first on the print copy and then on the computer, but I find that doing so results in a more comprehensive and much better final polish.

If you want, you can format the book in advance based on the final size of your book, such as a 6"x9" or 7"x10" book, and write your book using the final margins. Alternatively, you can use the usual 8 ½" x 11" letter-size manuscript and later format that to size.

As for how to write and edit your book, that could be the subject for a book by itself, so I will not cover that here. Suffice to say, your book should be well-written and carefully edited, so it is ready to be published as is.

## Writing the Book with a Consultant or Coach

If you want to write the book yourself, but need help with either the writing or keeping on schedule to write it, consider hiring a consultant or coach. Generally, the consultant will focus on the writing techniques, so you can write well, while the coach can help you stay on track and avoid any hurdles or distractions keeping you from the task. Though some consultants and coaches do both.

Usually, the consultant will be someone who has a track record in publishing their own books or has worked as an acquisitions or development editor in a company or as a freelance editor for writing clients. In this case, you are hiring the individual as a consultant to advise you rather than write your book for you, and the payment will generally reflect their expertise. Commonly, you can expect to spend between $150-300 an hour for a consultant.

A writing coach may have previous experience as a writer or editor, and some coaches also act as consultants. But often the coach is not an expert writer but has experience, and sometimes a credential, as a coach. There are a number of different types of coaches, including career coaches, life coaches, and business coaches, who focus on helping you develop your goals, create your plans, and put them into action -- in this case, writing your book. They also expect to check in with you regularly to see that you are achieving the timeline you have set up in consulting with them, and they help you overcome any issues or blocks standing in your way of putting your plan into action. Typically, coaches charge about $125-200 an hour.

## Hiring an Editor

Sometimes writers do their own editing, but some prefer to turn that over to an editor for the final editorial polish. The most common type of editor to do this is the line or copy editor, whose focus is on this detail work at the end of getting your manuscript ready for publication. Generally, such an editor charges about $35-60 an hour or gives you a per word amount based on their hourly rate.

This kind of editor is different from the developmental editor, who can help in organizing your manuscript and may get involved in rewriting or doing extensive editing which includes eliminating repetition, reorganizing copy for a better flow, and doing a final editorial polish. Commonly, such an editor will charge about $75 to $150 an hour.

## Hiring a Ghostwriter

If you don't want to write something yourself, that's where a ghostwriter can help. The ghostwriter is an uncredited writer who will write your book as a work-for-hire, where you have full control over the book. In some cases, you might later invite the ghostwriter to be a co-writer, if the ghostwriter already has a track record in the subject of your book. Or you might give the writer credit as a "with" writer, meaning that you are the author based on your expertise, while the "with" writer has written much or all of the book for you.

The particular arrangement depends on your agreement with the writer. Consider giving credit or not giving credit separate from your ownership and royalty arrangements. If writing your book is a straight ghostwriting job, the writer gets no credit, and this is a work-for-hire agreement, where you are fully in control, and the assignments of rights for any writing or creative input becomes yours upon full payments to the ghostwriter. Should you later decide to give the ghostwriter credit as a "with" or "and" writer, that doesn't affect any agreement you have about sharing royalties or not, though you can later modify your original agreement to share royalties, too, based on any percentage split you want. Use "with" if the writer has primarily used your material to write the book; use "and" if the writer has gone beyond being just a writer to contributing to the contents of the book.

Should the writer contribute substantially, an option is to make the writer a co-writer with an "and" designation, and then you can opt to share royalties or not. If you do share royalties, typically, any sharing doesn't occur until after you you have received back money you have paid the writer, per your agreement for writing the book.

In some cases, ghostwriters may ask for a formal agreement about their contribution in advance of writing the book, and sometimes that agreement will include a payment schedule in which they get 20-33% up front, another percentage after completing half of the manuscript, a further payment after completing three-quarters of the manuscript, and the rest of the money at the end. I generally prefer a retainer of 10-20% up front, and then work on a pay in advance or as you go arrangement.

I prefer to leave any shared royalties or credits open, since the author and ghostwriter can see how well they work together. This way, any agreement about being a co-writer or being credited as an "and" or "with" author is left open, based on negotiations after the ghostwriter has completed half or more of the project. The basic arrangement in this scenario is that the author retains full control and ghostwriter is fully paid for his or her work, with any other agreement negotiated down the road. This way you and the ghostwriter mutually decide if the ghostwriter should share credits or gain additional compensation through sharing in the project in some way.

# CHAPTER 10: FORMATTING YOUR BOOK FOR PUBLICATION

Once your book is written and fully edited, it is ready for publication. Depending on what platform you use for publishing, you need to format your document for publication. The Word document is one of the most popular formats, though sometimes you may need a PDF document, or you can use both. In some cases, a platform will want an epub document for an e-book, but commonly, the platform can convert your Word or PDF file into the required format.

One of the most popular platforms for print books which I use is CreateSpace, which has published over 1 million books for authors. They published nearly 300,000 books in 2014, about 425,000 books in 2015, and presumably even more books in 2016. So I'll focus on using CreateSpace, which has a free platform and over two dozen templates you can use for laying out your book. Once your book is published there, it is very easy to publish your book as an e-book on Kindle, which is a separate e-book publishing company owned by Amazon. After that, you can readily turn your book into an audiobook, once it is sold on Amazon, using ACX, another Amazon-owned company. While you can start by publishing an e-book on Kindle, I find it easier to start with a print copy on CreateSpace that can be converted into a Kindle e-book in minutes. It's also ideal to start with a print book, which you can show to others, if you are using your book to promote yourself or your business.

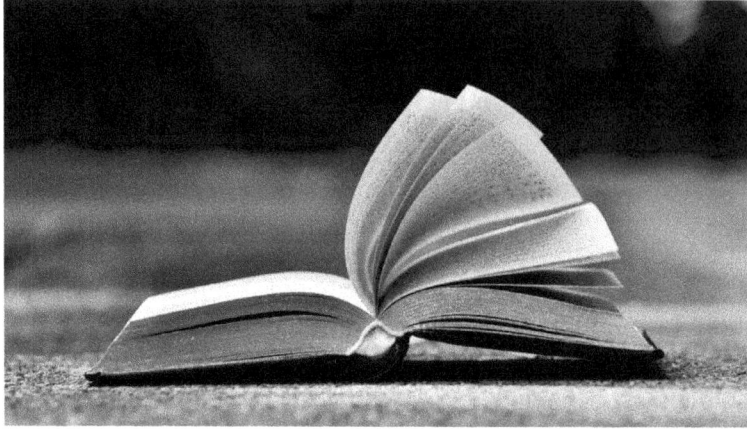

**The Steps to Preparing Your Document**

     To get started preparing your edited book for a print publication, create a final Word document or turn it into a PDF. Then, upload this document into CreateSpace. If you create a PDF, rather than use the "Save as PDF" option, it's best to print to a PDF to obtain a higher quality document. After you select print, select Adobe as your printer. Then, go to properties and change this from a Standard PDF to a PDF/X-1a2001, which is a higher quality PDF format designed for printing.

**Deciding on the Size of Your Book**

     You also have to set up the size of your document and select the minimum margins based on your book's page count. Most books are 6"x9", but if you're using many photographs or illustrations, I recommend a 7"x10" or 8"x10" size to show off your illustrations. If you are publishing a workbook where people will write or paste photos or illustrations in the book, I recommend an 8 ½" x11" format.

     Although you can choose any number of sizes, it's best not to select a custom size for your book, since you can't use one of the standard templates and have to have a custom cover created by a graphic designer, which becomes much more expensive, unless you can design the cover yourself.

**Setting Up Your Margins**

     Once you decide on the size of your book, set up your margins, which are affected by the number of pages. For most books, figure on a .75" margin on the right and left, and at least a .75 margin on the top and bottom, though I prefer a 1" top and bottom margin to give the book more white space around the text, so it is easier to read. If you have a longer book with 400 or more pages, you need larger margins, such as 1" on the right and left, which is required by CreateSpace. This additional margin size is required for binding the book together in the manufacturing process.

For certain types of books you may want even larger margins, such as if you are featuring poems or short copy for a children's book, since you have much shorter copy and a larger font size on a page. The wider margins help to feature this text, and it looks better with this extra white space around it. For example, I've been doing a series of kid's books where I use 1.5" margins.

## Determining the Type Font and Size

You can choose from a wide range of standard and special typefaces, although some typefaces may not be permitted, due to copyright issues. And some may be relatively rare, so another typeface has to be substituted for them. If there are such issues, you may find that you can't convert a Word document with a particular font into a PDF, and the CreateSpace platform will normally reject that font, too, and advise you that you can't use that type. The easy solution is to choose another typeface and globally change the font in your manuscript.

One of the most common and popular fonts for books is Times New Roman, which is what I use.

As for the size of the type, the standard for most books is 12 pt. Times New Roman, though for some short books, it may be better to use a 13 pt. type, so the book runs a little longer. In the case of very short books, such as books with poems or quotes, or children's picture books, 14 point type with a wider than normal margin is ideal, since you have only a small amount of text on a page.

## Using Footnotes, End Notes, and References

If you are doing a book with references, there are three ways to do this.
- Put the footnotes at the bottom of the page.
- Put endnotes at the end of the book.
- Put endnotes at the end of each chapter.

Whichever approach you use, include a bibliography with the cited references in a "Bibliography" section at the end of the book. If you list additional references you haven't used, include them in a separate "Additional References" or "Resources" section following the "Bibliography" section.

The easiest approach is to put the footnotes at the bottom of the page, since you can readily see what footnotes go with each number in the text. Alternatively, you can turn the footnotes into endnotes at the end of the book with a click of a button. Both the footnotes and endnotes will have the same number.

To put the end notes at the back of each chapter, the style many traditional publishers prefer, you have to first separate each chapter into a separate file with end notes at the end of the chapter. If you still have footnotes, turn them into end notes for that chapter. Then, print each chapter separately as a PDF. Next, print the front section of the book, which might include the title page, copyright page, any acknowledgements, and the table of contents as a separate file. Then, print the last sections of the book which might include the bibliography, additional references, author's bio and contact information as another file. Finally, combine each of the PDFs in the correct order. Start with the first file; then add each subsequent file to the complete document file. You can't combine the files like this in Word, because all the end notes will be continuous at the end of the book, rather than at the end of in each chapter.

## Adding Testimonials or Acknowledgments

If you have testimonials or acknowledgments, you can feature them on a page or series of pages in the beginning of the book. You can also use one or two of them for your back cover copy, which you can either write directly into the template for the back cover or create as a separate document and copy and paste into the template.

## Adding a Title and Copyright Page

You need a Title Page in the front of the book. This should have the same Title and Author information as on the front cover, and if you have a subtitle, include this, too. If you want, you can include your company and contact information on the bottom of the Title Page, or put this on a separate page in the back of the book.

You should also have a Copyright Page, which usually goes on the back of the Title Page, or you can skip a page and put the copyright page there. The copyright form will look something like this, which is the same as the copyright notice I include in the front of my books. The "All rights reserved" section is basic boilerplate. You can use any kind of wording, and you can use a shorter version if you wish. The most important part of the notice is the name of your book, the copyright date, and your name or company name, whichever is the copyright holder.

# NAME OF YOUR BOOK

## Author's Bio

The "Author's Bio" is optional, though generally you want to include a bio of yourself, your company, or both. Preferably, keep this to a single page.

## Contact Information

Commonly, the contact information goes on its own page in the back of the book, though some authors put this on the Title Page or Copyright Page. I generally put this information in the back, though where it goes is up to you.

## Creating the Table of Contents

It's easy to create the Table of Contents in Word. You just go to the "References" tab, select the "Table of Contents" link, and set up the table of contents there. You can choose among different styles, and if there is extra spacing, go to the "paragraph" setting and select "single" to get rid of the spacing between lines. You can similarly change the type size, if the type is too small or large. I generally prefer Times New Roman with 12 pt. type and single spacing for the Table of Contents, unless it's a short book where I have used 13 pt. or 14 pt. type.

To create each entry, headings, and subheadings in your text, indicate the heading level by highlighting the header and choosing the correct heading level. Generally, each chapter heading will be Header or Heading 1. The subheadings will be Header or Heading 2. Unless it's a long book, there is no need to create additional subheads under your subheadings. The Table of Contents will automatically be set up based on these headings and the page numbers.

If you add any material after you create the headings, update the Table of Contents, so you have the latest headers and page numbers in your Word document or PDF, when you upload it into the CreateSpace platform or whatever platform you are using.

## Starting Key Sections on Odd Numbered Pages

After everything else is ready to go, set up your pages, so that your chapter headings and any major categories in your book appear on an odd number page. The reason for this is that when your book is published, the odd numbered pages will appear on the right, while the even number pages will appear on the left, so they print out as the back of the odd number pages. By setting up the beginning of each chapter in this way, as you read a print book, the chapter headings and major categories will always be on the right.

Accordingly, as you go through your book, add in or take out blank pages as necessary, so these headings and categories will be on odd number pages. For example, the following pages should be on odd number pages.

- Title Page
- Table of Contents
- Foreword or Preface (if you have this)
- Introduction (if you have this)
- Chapters 1, 2, 3, etc.
- Bibliography (if you have this)
- Additional References or Resources (if you have this)
- Author's Bio (if you have this)
- Contact Information (if you have this)

In the event your book features photos or illustrations with copy, if the pictures are on a separate page from the text, its best to feature them on the right, with the copy on the left. If publishing a children's book, put the illustrations on the right if the copy and text are on different pages. If the copy and illustration are on the same page, start each chapter as an odd page as previously described.

## Creating a Cover Page

You can either create your cover using a CreateSpace template or create a cover using the specs provided by CreateSpace based on your book dimensions and page count. If you use a template, fill in the requested information for the title, subtitle if there is one, author bio, back cover copy, and in some templates, you can add in an author photo and company logo. Alternately, you can use a template to upload a completed front page or both a front page and back cover, scaled to the appropriate dimension. Or if you prefer, you can create a complete cover according to the indicated specs, based on the book's size and number of pages, which affect the size of the spine.

# CHAPTER 11: PUBLISHING YOUR BOOK

Today, there are five main formats for publishing your book. I'll describe them briefly here.

**The Five Main Publishing Formats**

- <u>Print-On-Demand</u>. You create a master file, and can order as many copies as you want whenever you want them. The most popular platform, which I've been using, is CreateSpace.

- <u>E-Book</u>. The most popular platform that everyone knows about is Kindle, which is a division of Amazon. You can easily publish with a Word document or PDF, and sometimes with a few other publishing formats. Another e-book platform is Smashwords, which sends a master file to about a dozen different platforms. The Smashword platform is a little more complicated to set up, since you have to format a Word document a certain way and adhere to restrictions on the size of the type, spacing between paragraphs, and other style requirements. This formatting takes about five or six hours for an average document. Given these requirements, I haven't used Smashwords recently, but it's another good platform.

Audiobooks. You can create an audiobook and sell it on a number of different platforms, if you know what you are doing to get good quality sound. One of the most popular distribution channels is Audible, and if you're published on Amazon, there is an easy way to create your audiobook. You can go to the ACX platform, click "This is my book," and fill in copyright and other information about it. Then, you can either find a narrator or narrate the book yourself, but you have to know what you're doing in order to meet certain technical specs. For example, you have to have to have five seconds of room tone in the beginning of the book, can't have any background sound, no mic clicks, have the right sound level, and more.

Thus, unless you know what you're doing and have the facilities to create a perfect audiobook without sound interference, don't do it. Just get a narrator. ACX has hundreds of narrators on the platform, and it links the narrators and authors together. Once your book is listed on the platform, you can hire somebody for about $100 to $200 per finished hour. Or you can partner up with a narrator, which is what I have been doing. I look for a narrator who is willing to split the royalties. Under this partnership arrangement, the audiobook becomes exclusive to ACX, which distributes on Audible, Amazon, and iTunes. I have over 50 books that I turned into audio books using this system.

I'd recommend creating an audiobook for any book, since I have found that my audiobooks sell better than my paperback books, although I originally thought of audiobooks as a side venture which I started doing just for fun. So far, I've sold 625 audio books in about 9 months with almost no promotion. My biggest seller, *Homicide by the Rich and Famous,* has sold 185 copies, and it's a long book – about 400 print page and 10 hours as an audio book, though most audiobooks are short – about an hour or two to narrate 10,000 to 20,000 words. By contrast, I only sell a few dozen copies a month for about 100 books on CreateSpace and Amazon. This lower sales of print books is because more and more people are listening to audiobooks, such as when they are driving, commuting, or flying somewhere, and they are reading fewer printed books.

A PDF. This is where you offer your book as a PDF, which customers can download or open online to read. You can sell these through online platforms for digital products, or offer them through your website. After people buy the book, they download it or read it online. The profit potential is huge, because once the book is created, it's very inexpensive to send it as an attachment or provide a download link for the book. The only cost is the time it takes to process the order and send the file, although if you have enough orders, it pays to automate this process with an autoresponder – about $20 a month to start.

PowerPoint or Video. You can turn your PowerPoint presentations into videos and sell those through a platform like Pivotshare. Ideally, you can use your PowerPoint or video for online courses for your book, which is the next step that I'm doing. I'm turning my print-on-demand and e-books into PowerPoints, and then turning these into videos. I'm doing the videos by putting the main points of each chapter on PowerPoint slides. Then, I talk about each slide while recording my talk as a voiceover. Or you can take an audio file with your narration and combine it with the PowerPoint using a video editing program like Camtasia.

Once you create your videos, you use them as a series of modules in which you generally introduce each video by talking into a camera or smartphone, after which you show your videos created from your PowerPoints. Viewers who want more information, can then download a PDF with the chapters of your book corresponding to each module or can download a PDF with the whole book.

## Getting a Copyright for Your Book

Your book is automatically copyrighted when you create it whether you have a copyright notice on it or not. But putting a notice on your book shows you want the book to be copyrighted by you, not created for the public domain.

When you create an audiobook, the narrator reads the copyright notice aloud, with a copyright for you as the author and a copyright for the narrator in the audiobook. Some audiobooks have the copyright notice in the beginning; others at the end. You can use your more detailed copyright notice in your book, or preferably write a shortened version where you only indicate the Copyright, date, title of the book, and your name. ACX has a standard copyright notice for narrators to read, too. The print, audio, and video versions of the book all have separate copyrights, just like each one has its own ISBN.

## Getting an ISBN

You need an ISBN to distribute your book. An ISBN stands for International Standard Book Number, a 10 or 13-digit number which identifies each book and edition of a book, as well as any book-like product, such as an audiobook. Since 1970, each published book has a unique ISBN, and beginning in 2007, assigned ISBNs changed from 10 to 13 digits. You need a different ISBN for every version of your book.

You can get a free ISBN when you publish on CreateSpace, although then CreateSpace will be listed as the publisher on Amazon, which is a clear signal this is a self-published book, even though you can put your publisher name on the book cover. You can get your own publisher listing, but it now costs $99 for that ISBN, though that used to be only $10. An alternative, which is especially useful if you publish multiple books, is to buy a package of 10 or more ISBNs from Bowker (http://www.bowker.com/products/ISBN-US.html), which is the only official source of ISBNs in the United States. The cost is $125 for 1 ISBN or $295 for Bowker's most popular package of 10 ISBNs. Then, you can bring that ISBN to CreateSpace or whatever platform you use for publishing your book.

**Pricing Your Book**

Whatever publishing platform you use, you need to think about pricing. Set a price that is competitive, based on the costs of publishing the book. A good price point is around $7.95 to $14.95 for a shorter book of about 50-150 pages; about $9.95-$19.95 for a longer book of over 150 pages, as long as this is printed with a black and white interior. You have to increase the price for color. Figure on about $3 to $4 more for a book under 100 pages; $5-10 more for a book of 150 pages; and the price goes up exponentially from there.

For example, I had a 350 page book with about 200 photos, which I could sell for as little as $19.95 if I had black and white photos; but if wanted to publish them in color, I had to price the book for at least $74.00. Needless to say, I only published the book with black and white photos and set the pricing at $24.95.

If you publish with CreateSpace, they give you a minimum price you can charge, which is about two and half times what it costs you to buy the book. For example, with a short book of under 100 pages, I can buy the book for $2.15. The minimum retail is $5.58, and I can price the book at anything I want over that amount. I usually price the book at $7.95 if it is about 50 pages; at $8.95 if the book is about 75 pages; $9.95 if it's between 76 and 100 pages; more if longer.

In the case of e-books, a popular price level is $2.99, though if you want to encourage sales for a new book to help build your name and brand, try pricing your book at $.99 or $1.99. If it is a longer book with very helpful how-to or financial information, you can price it higher, say $4.99 to $9.99.

Typical prices for audiobooks range from $3.95-$8.95, depending on the length of the recording. If you publish through the ACX platform, distributed through Audible, Amazon, and iTunes, the company will set the price for you.

**Purchasing Your Book**

Some companies that publish, distribute, and market print books for self-publishers have a minimal purchase requirement as part of their package, such as buying 25, 50, or 100 books or more. Other companies offer varying prices for individual purchases. Plan to get at least 2 or 3 copies for display; more if you plan to sell books at workshops, seminars, speaking engagements or other events.

Compare the costs if you are looking at different self-publishing packages. I use CreateSpace, a print-on-demand publisher, with no minimum requirement and lower per book costs compared to other self-publishing companies.

# CHAPTER 12: CREATING A POD BOOK: PUBLISHING ON CREATE SPACE

There are dozens of printers and print-on-demand publishers that are turning manuscripts into books. Among some of the best known ones are Lulu, BookBaby, Outskirt Press, Trafford Publishing, iUniverse, AuthorHouse, and Xlibris. A number of publishers, such as Wiley and Hay House, have set up self-publishing arms, which are separate from the company's royalty published books. Additionally, book packaging companies such as the Jenkins Group, and local book designers and publishers help with self-publishing, too. Many of these options can be fairly expensive, starting at around $1500 for designing and producing your book, plus an additional charge for more than 5 or 10 book copies. You can readily find these publishing companies online for more details and comparison shopping.

## Using the CreateSpace Platform

My favorite publishing platform is CreateSpace, which is part of Amazon. The platform itself is free, and it offers about 30 cover templates which you can use to design your front and back cover, although you can design your own cover or hire a graphics designer, as long as you follow the company's specs. Once you set up your account and choose your ISBN – provided by CreateSpace, under your name with a CreateSpace ISBN, or you bring your own ISBN, you enter details about your book. These include the title and any subtitle, author's name, book size, background color, text, paper stock, and a publisher logo if you have one. Additionally you add a book description, back cover copy, and include an optional author's photo and bio. After you upload your interior file, which can be in a Word document or a PDF file, you are done with the basics.

Then, you have to set the pricing for the U.S. and other countries, which has to be at least a minimum amount, based on the number of pages, whether in color or black and white. Additionally, you have to set up the distribution, which initially includes the CreateSpace bookstore, Amazon, and Amazon affiliates worldwide. You can set up expanded distribution through bookstores, libraries, and academic institutions.

You can easily make changes in almost everything except the ISBN number for a title. Even after the book is published, you can withdraw it to make further changes, such as changing the title if potential customers don't like it. You can submit a different cover photo or back cover. if you come up with a better design or want to make back-cover copy changes to better describe the book or have changes in your work or life.

A big advantage of the CreateSpace platform is that it is free. Also much of the process of submitting your interior file or submitting all your files for review is automated, so it can take just a minute to submit the manuscript and less than a day for the staff to review and approve it. If it isn't approved, the staff will explain what's wrong and suggest guidelines for you to review to fix the problem.

**How to Publish Your Book on CreateSpace**

Although CreateSpace provides detailed guidelines for what to do, these sometimes can be confusing, so you might want a professional's help to navigate this, which is something my company, Changemakers Publishing, does. Contact us at www.changemakerspublishing.com for details.

To illustrate how to publish your book, I have included screen shots of the basic steps involved in publishing it. To begin, set up an account, which includes providing your name, email, password, bank, credit card, and tax information. Then, open up your Member Dashboard, where you click "Add New Title" for each book you want to publish. Initially, no titles are listed, though once you start publishing books, they will be listed under their title name, status, title number, and a link to click to place your orders.

Since I'm using my account to illustrate, the dashboard includes other titles, along with the royalty balance from the US, UK, and countries in Europe.

Once you have your account set up and click "Add and New Project," you will be asked to put in basic information about it, including its name and type of project. I'll use the name of the book which will include this chapter: "The Complete Guide to Using Email Marketing to Promote Your Book or Business." Since this will be a paperback, I'll check that. You have to put in your initial title to get started, but you can change it later if you come up with a better name.

Then, click "Get Started" for the "Guided" option, since you want help in going through the process. This will take you to the "Title Screen," where you can add a subtitle if you have one, along with the name of the author or authors. If more than one author, click "Add Contributors" and provide the additional information. If you want to include an illustrator, list him or her here. You can leave the other screens about whether this is a series, the language, and the publication's date blank. Here's a filled out example of this screen below.

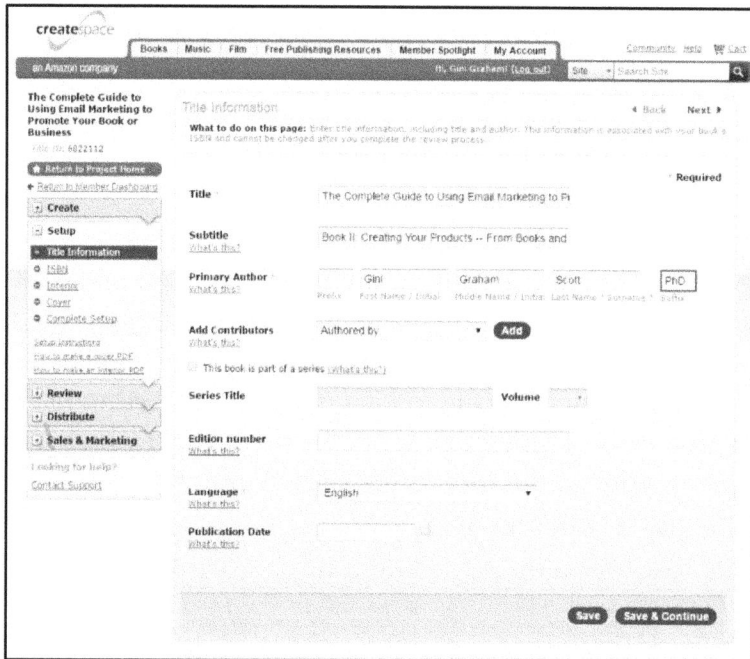

Hit "Save and Continue" to go on, which will take you to the ISBN screen. I recommend getting the free CreateSpace ISBN, which you can use in all sales venues. It will show up as a CreateSpace book, though you can put your own logo on the back cover. It is much more expensive to get another type of ISBN. It costs $99 to get your own ISBN through CreateSpace, and it costs $125 to get one ISBN or $250 for 10 ISBNs from Bowker, the official ISBN provider, to get your ISBN there. If you sell PDFs direct to customers through other sales channels, you don't need an ISBN. So in getting started, it makes sense to take the free option. Once you choose this option, you'll see an explanation about what it means to choose a free ISBN, so you can still choose another option. Otherwise, click "Assign Free ISBN," which is then locked in for this book.

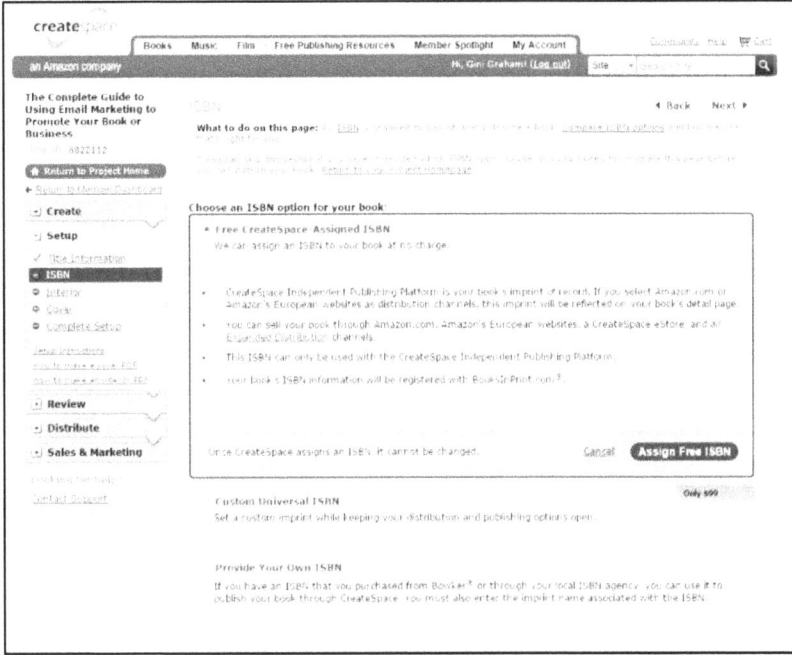

You can always republish this book with another ISBN, if you want to make any updates or variations on the book – such as having one book with color photos and another with black and white photos.

Here's the notice you get after you select a CreateSpace ISBN. It shows the number of the ISBN and the lock symbol indicating that the ISBN number is forever tied to this book.

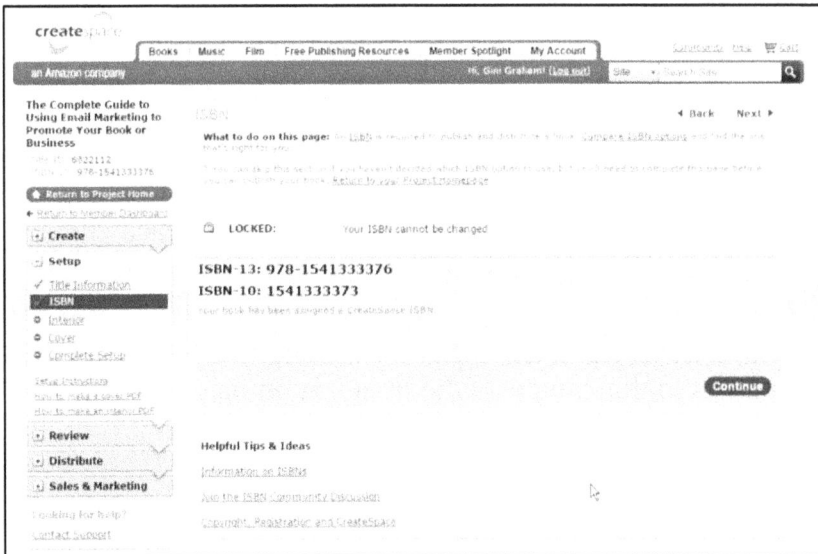

## Creating Your Interior

After you hit continue, you next have choices to make about the interior. The default setting is a 6" x 9" book with a black and white interior on white paper, although you can change the size, color, and paper stock. Unless you have a good reason, it's best to stick with the defaults, since these are the most popular book formats. However, if you will be using color photos or illustrations, choose color, and then you might want to choose a larger size to show off the photos. That's what I did in this book series, since I want to use a number of color photos to better illustrate the points I am making. So in this case, the books will all be 7" x 10," and the images will be in full color.

As you can see, I had plenty of options to choose from. I could even create my custom size. But it is better to stick to a more common standard for more distribution options, since distribution is more limited for books in unusual sizes.

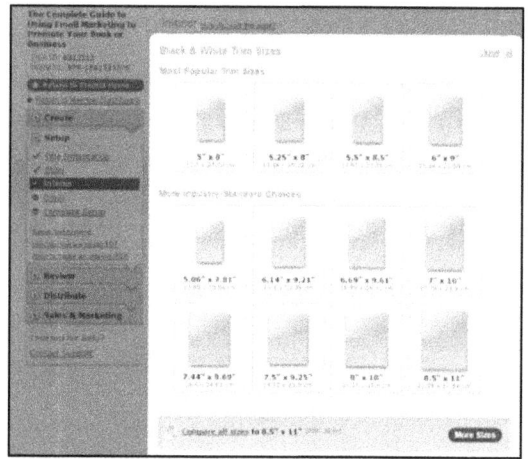

Although not required, it is a good idea to begin each chapter on an odd number page, so it shows up on the right side of the book after it is printed. Add extra pages as needed, so your chapter will be on the right hand side. Ideally, any images should be included on the same page as the text which relates to this image. If the image is on its own page, I recommend putting the image on an odd number page, so it is on the right side, which is more readily viewed by the reader.

createspace

Books    Music    Film    Free Publishing Resources    Member Spotlight    My Account

an Amazon company                                          Hi, Gini Graham! (Log out)    Site

The Complete Guide to
Using Email Marketing to
Promote Your Book or
Business

6822112
978-15-1333376

★ Return to Project Home
← Return to Member Dashboard

⊡ Create

⊟ Setup
  ✓ Title Information
  ✓ ISBN
  ► Interior
  ○ Cover
  ○ Complete Setup

⊡ Review

⊡ Distribute

⊡ Sales & Marketing

**Interior Type**

Black & White        Full Color

**Paper Color**

                     Not Available

White                Cream

**Trim Size**

7" x 10"
Choose a Different Size

↓ Download a Word® Template

→ Estimate your book's manufacturing costs

Choose how you'd like to submit your interior:

**Upload your Book File**
You can upload your work as a print ready .pdf, .doc, .docx, or .rtf. Your page count will be detected and an automated print check will run once your upload is complete. You'll be able to see any issues online using the Interior Reviewer tool.

**Talk with us about Professional Design Services**    Starting at $199
Let us design and format your manuscript. Our experienced team can help with fonts, margins, chapter headings, and other eye-catching details to enhance the professional appearance of your book.

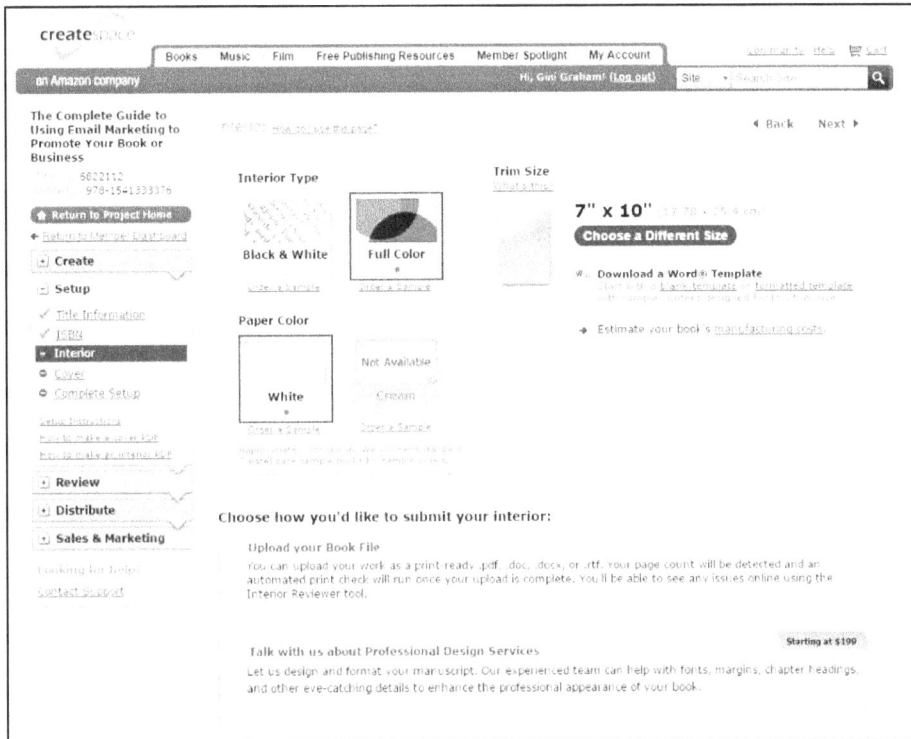

Once the interior file is ready with your completed manuscript in a Word or PDF file, you can upload it. Your manuscript should be formatted in the correct size and margins for it to be accepted. If not, the manuscript review process will identify if there are any errors, so you can correct any serious errors or let them go if less important. For example, a common caution occurs when you have less than 300 dpi images, which is the usual standard for printing, where "dpi" stands for "dots per inch." The more dots or pixels per inch, the higher the resolution, and images may become blurry if the resolution is too low and the image size too large. However, today, many individuals use cameras on cell phones with a lower resolution, and commonly images on the web are at 72 dpi, so the book can be printed with lower resolution images, though you will get a warning that these images are less than the full 300 dpi standard.

Should you forget to change the letter-sized Word or PDF document to a smaller size to match your choice, you will get a warning that the text or images in the manuscript are not the correct size so they overlap the margins. In this case, one fix is to go back to the original Word document and format the manuscript to the correct size there, including reducing the size of any photos as necessary. The other fix, if you have a PDF document, which can't be reduced in size, is to save the PDF as a JPEG, which will turn each page into a JPEG image, which is numbered in sequence. Then, you can insert each JPEG as a picture in the same order in the original document (and you will have the page number on each page to guide you, although you can crop this out of the JPEG and put the page number in the Word document). Once you have a Word document with all of the needed images, you can save or print it as a PDF in this new size and upload that.

To illustrate, I've uploaded a 7" x 10" document with color photos using the "Browse" button, since this is the format I have chosen for this book. After I hit "Save", CreateSpace uploads the file, processes it, and does an automated print check, which takes a few minutes. If you wish, you can start working on your cover, and CreateSpace will notify you when the print check is done.

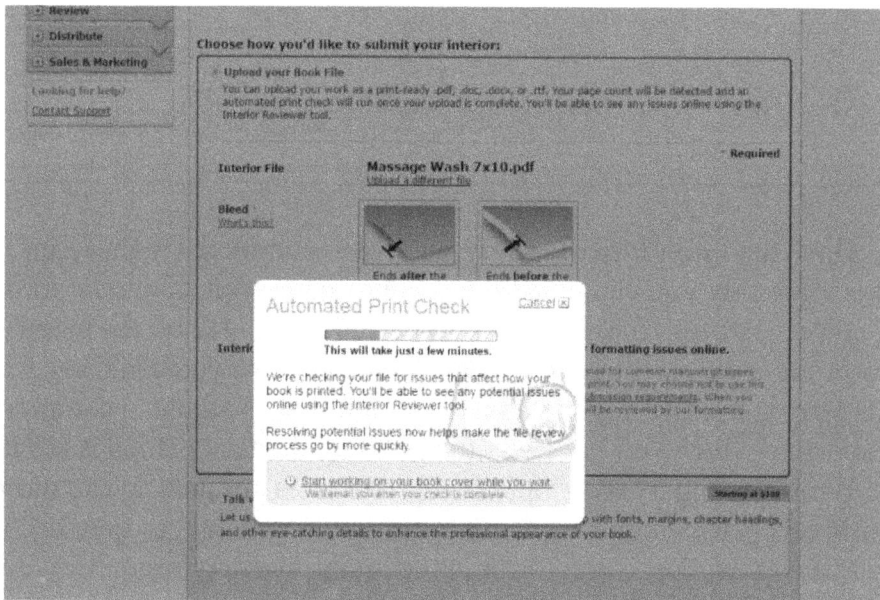

Once the print check is complete, you will get a notice if CreateSpace found any issues with your file, so you can see what they are and correct them. Or, if you have that option, you can decide to ignore any of these issues and publish despite that interior problem. For example, here I have been notified that the print check found one issue with my file.

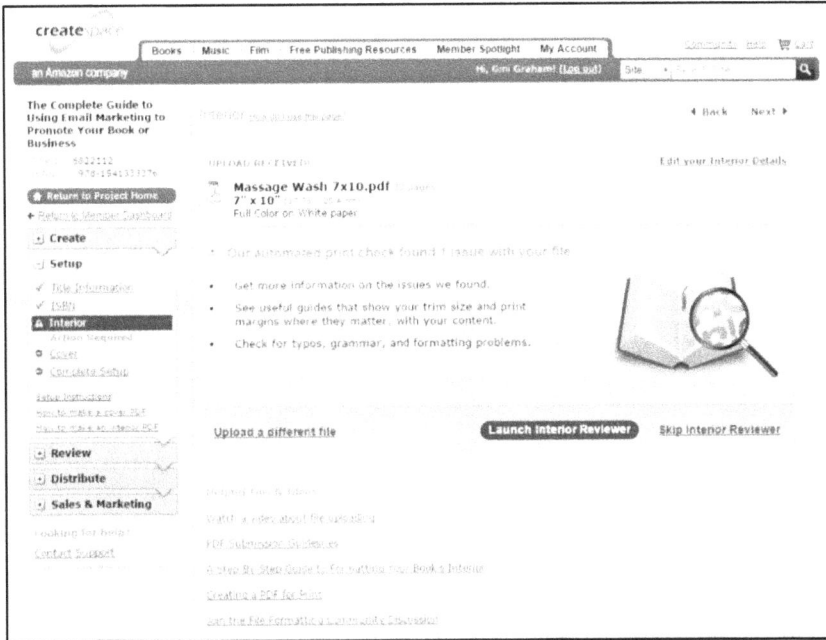

When you launch the interior reviewer, you will see what this issue was when you flip through the pages. If you have to make a correction, you can always upload a different file, such as if you make changes in this file or use another file.

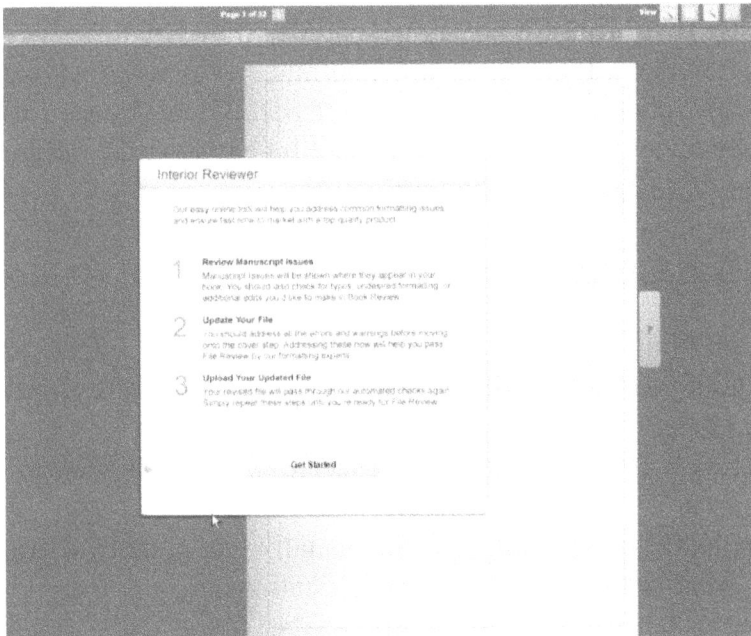

For example, after I clicked the sliders to flip from page to page, any problem on that page is indicated by a small red and yellow marker. Then I can decide if this is not a serious issue, so I can ignore it, or if I have to fix the file or upload another. In this case, the issue was the lower dpi images, which I ignored in publishing the book. Though I used the interior file from another book to demonstrate the process, since I'm still writing this book, this example illustrates the review process that all books go through.

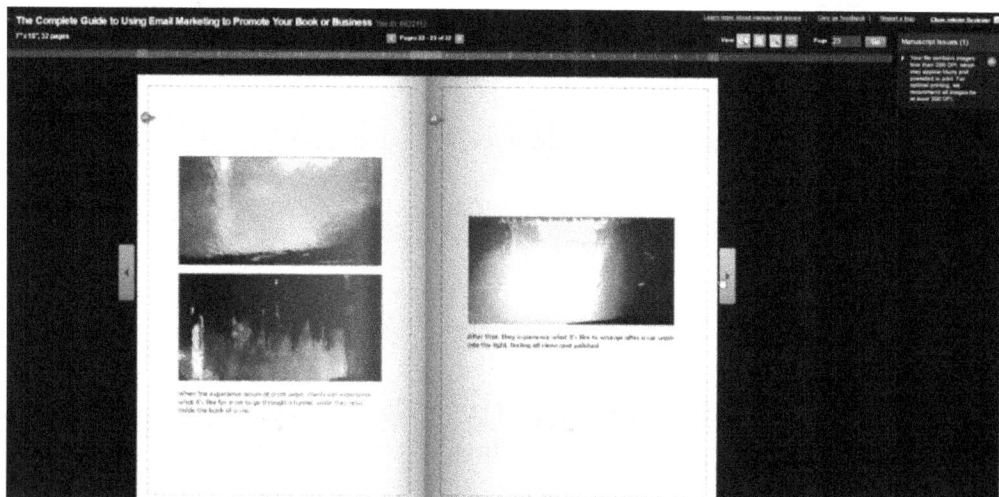

After reviewing for any issues indicated by CreateSpace – or any problem, I noticed, I hit "Save and Continue," which allows me to ignore the issues and continue or upload another file, in which case I would go through the review process again. Once I hit "Save and Continue," I'm back at the "Create a Cover" screen.

## Creating Your Cover

In building your cover, you have three options:
- build your cover online, which involves using the template and adding or changing information to create a book cover,
- choose a professional design service starting at $399 to create the cover,
- upload a completed PDF file, usually one done by a graphics designer, which exactly meets the specifications.

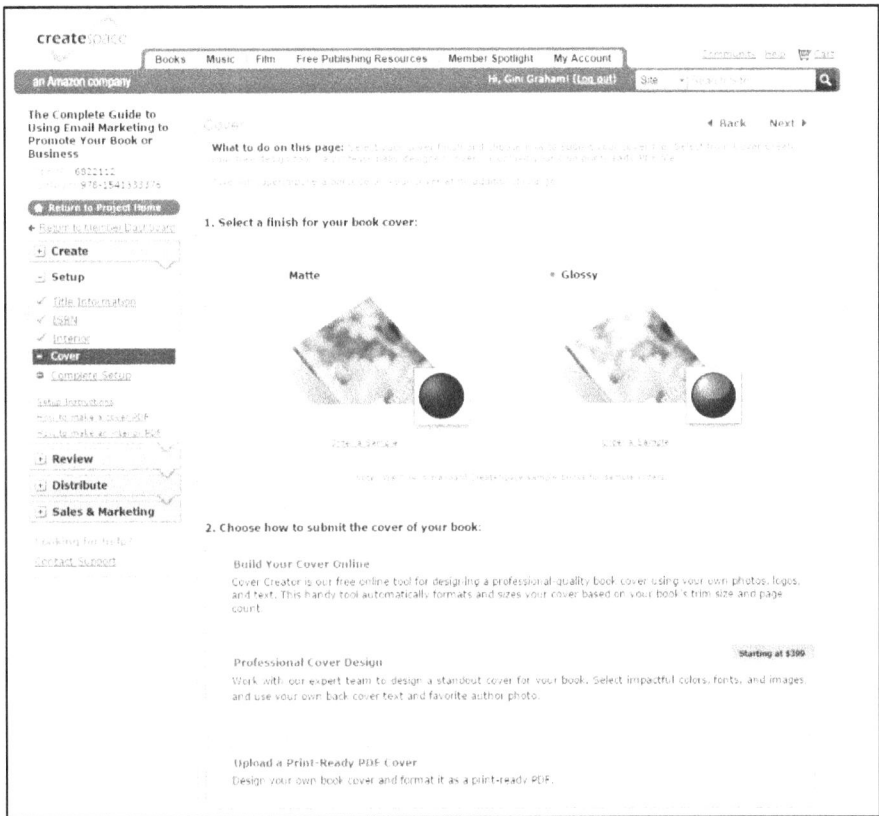

Normally, you want to build your cover online, because using a template is the less expensive and easiest way to go, since you just need a cover photo or illustration which costs from nothing if you have the picture, to a few bucks from a stock photo house. The alternatives of having a CreateSpace designer or outside designer will be much more expensive. Figure on about $500-1000 for a designer to create an original cover.

Once you choose "Build Your Cover Online," you choose a design template and can modify it. You have 30 templates to choose from.

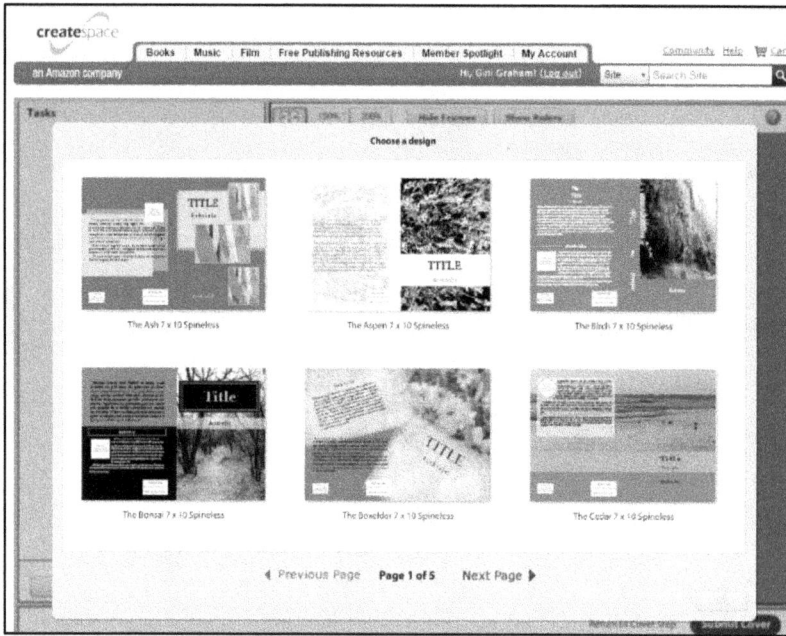

I'll choose the Oak, since I have a line of books using this template. For consistency, it's a good idea to use the same style for a series of books or for all of your books to build your brand.

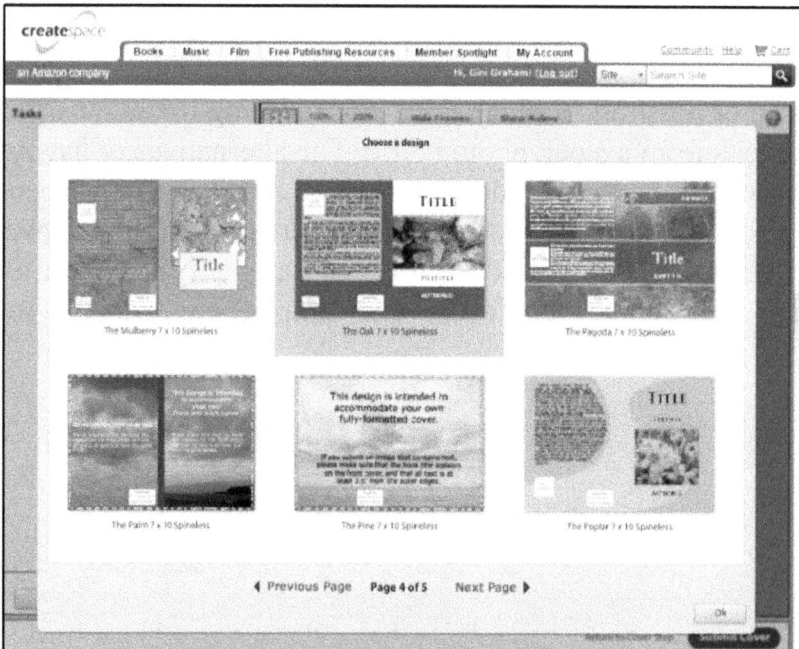

Next, you have a number of choices to modify the template. These include changing the color of the background and fonts, adding an author bio and photo, and uploading a publisher logo or not. You also have to write your back cover copy, and sometimes you can modify the overall theme. With most templates, you can also add a front cover photo, which is a very important choice, since it is a major factor in sales. Normally, the photo will feature one strong image, but you can create a composite image, using a program like PhotoShop. Here's what my cover looks like after I made all these adjustments, except for adding the back cover copy.

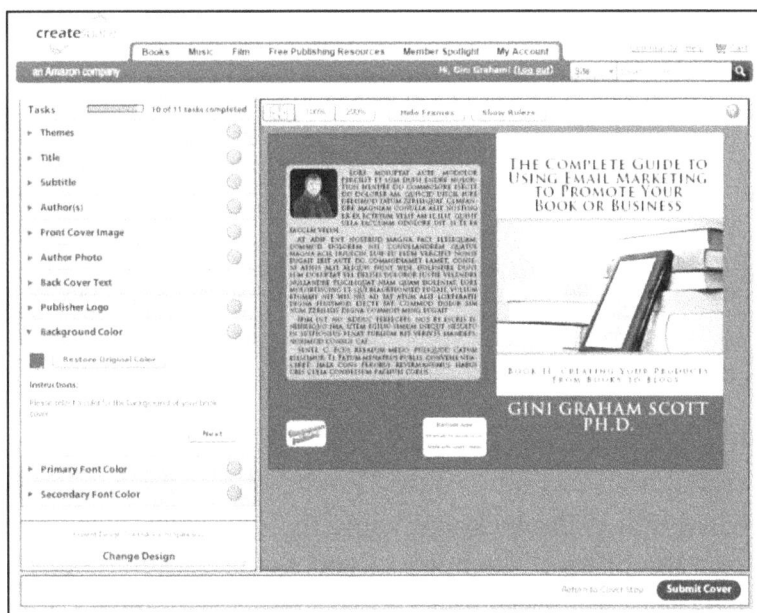

If you are creating your own cover or working with an outside designer, you will submit your cover – in this case as a PDF – following detailed specs on the cover size and layout, based on the size of the book and the number of pages. As the above design indicates, the back cover is on the left; then there is a spine with its exact width determined by the thickness of the paper and the number of pages; and the front cover is on the right. You will get the precise specs from the publisher and have to follow them exactly, or you have to do your cover again. For instance, I had one client who didn't do this and ended up with the front cover on the left and back cover on the right, which might be fine for a poster, but not for a cover for a published book. So, of course, the review team sent back the cover and she had to redo it.

Then, you set up your distribution channels, which not only include Amazon in the U.S. and Europe and the CreateSpace store, but can also include bookstores, online retailers, libraries, and academic institutions. The CreateSpace platform makes it easy to set up these distribution arrangements with the click of a few buttons. Plus you can add in information about your book, including a description, your author's bio, and keywords.

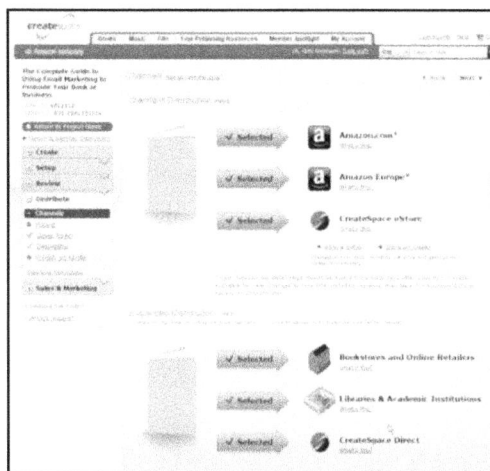

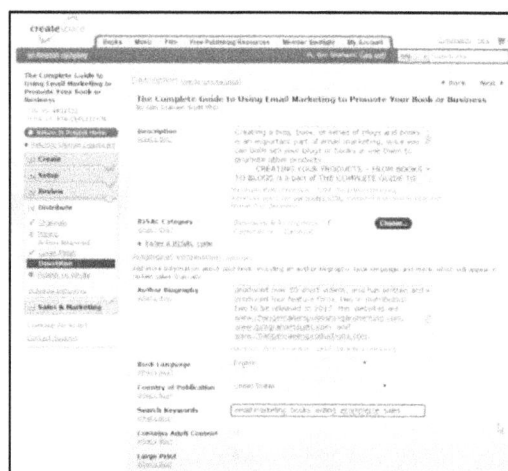

Finally, determine pricing. You have to at least price the book at the minimum for that book, which is based on the size of the book, number of pages, and whether it is in black and white or color. Plus CreateSpace adds a mark-up from the price of the book to you as the author. Using color will substantially increase the price, but choose color if you have color photos and illustrations, which are an important part of the book. The mark-up for sales will typically be about 2 ½ times the cost to you.

For example, a small book of up to about 75 pages will be about $2.15 when you order it, but the minimum price will be about $5.50. If you publish the book in color, the minimum price will be about $3.50 with a minimum price of $9.00. You can mark-up the price however you want, though think strategically. If you plan to primarily use the book for promotional purposes, keep the price low; but if you want to combine online sales with turning the material in the book into an introductory course at a reduced price, price the book higher, so your price for the course will be lower than the book in order to encourage more sign-ups. Whatever price you set, CreateSpace will convert this into other currencies for sales in other markets.

70

For example, since I am mainly planning to use these email marketing books for promotional purposes, I have set a low price of $9.95, since the minimum price is $9.15. I have used the common pricing for books which ends in $.95. Once I set the price, the platform fills in the royalty for the different sales platforms, as well as sets the sales price in the currencies for other countries

The final step after filling in all of the required information is to submit your files for review. Once you submit your files, you will usually hear back within 24 hours, and if your book is accepted, you review the proof. After you approve it, your book will be published immediately on CreateSpace, and it will be available on Amazon within a few hours.

Should there be any problems with your manuscript, such as a mismatch between your title on the cover and your title page, the review will catch this and advise you, so you can make the correction. Then, you have to submit your files again. If you still want to make changes, you can do so now and resubmit your files. In fact, even after your book is published, you can make changes, where you unpublish your original version, resubmit your interior and cover files again, and go through the same approval process.

Should you decide to self-publish with another print-on-demand publishers, you will go through much the same steps, though the particular platform for entering information will differ.

Since you have a non-exclusive publishing agreement with CreateSpace, you can always publish this material anywhere else, as well as remove it from the CreateSpace platform at any time.

# CHAPTER 13: CREATING AN EBOOK: PUBLISHING ON KINDLE

The two main ways of publishing e-books are as PDFs and as e-books available from e-book platforms, such as Kindle and Smashwords, the two most popular platforms.

While PDFs might be used to create the interiors for traditional and self-published books, they also might be considered e-books, in that they are used by e-mail marketers in several ways:

- providing gifts as lead magnets to build lists and sell other books and courses,
- providing additional information for courses and trainings,
- being sold as a digital product available online.

As e-books, they are generally provided to customers as email attachments or are available for downloading from a website or online delivery service, such as Dropbox or Hightail. Or often in online sales, they are delivered automatically by an autoresponder, such as AWeber or GetResponse, or they may be provided to purchasers through an online sales portal, which offers products and services from multiple vendors, such as ClickBank, JVZoo, WarriorPlus, and Zaxaa. Many PDFs are also sold as PLR (private label rights) books, which customers can use for their own purposes by relabeling or freely adapting the material in these books, which are supposed to be copyright free. Sometimes, though, these articles have the authors' names and copyright notices. Since online filters for plagiarism can identify duplicate copies of a copied work, it is best to revise and adapt any material you want to use to make it your own.

## Using PDF or Word Documents

However they are created, PDFs can be used for stand-alone sales, and they are ideal for this purpose if you are using them to offer unique targeted copy for a particular market, such as sales materials for the online marketing community or new equipment for furniture makers. Also the PDFs are ideal ways of featuring or summarizing information from a training program or boot camp.

Alternatively, PDFs, along with Word and text documents, can be used to create e-books which can be read on the Kindle and other mobile devices or tablets with an e-reader app.  One advantage of using more popular e-book publishing platforms, like Kindle, Smashwords, or Draft2Digital, is they also provide distribution.  For example, Smashwords has distribution arrangements with about two dozen online book sellers, including iBooks, Baker & Taylor, Kobo, Scribd, while Draft2Digital has partnerships with Apple, Baker & Taylor, Kobo, and Scribd, while Draft2Digital has partnerships with Apple, Barnes & Noble, Kobo, Inktera, Scribd, Baker & Taylor, and several others. Kindle books automatically get distributed through Amazon, as well as through other international distributors.

One advantage of publishing with any of these platforms is they are non-exclusive, so you can publish the same books on other platforms, though some distributors, such as Apple, will restrict sales to only one of these platforms.  You can see these three main platforms below.

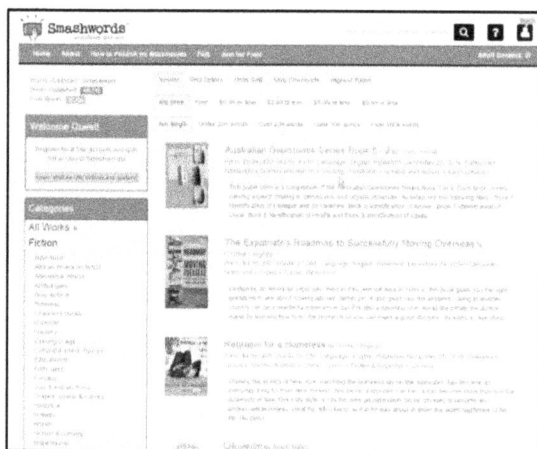

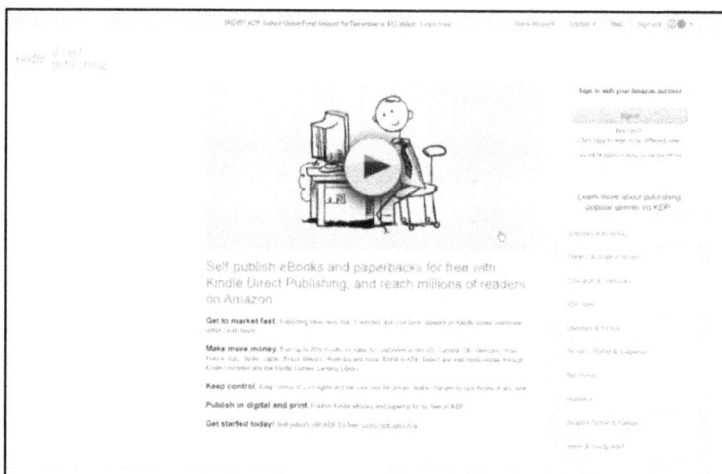

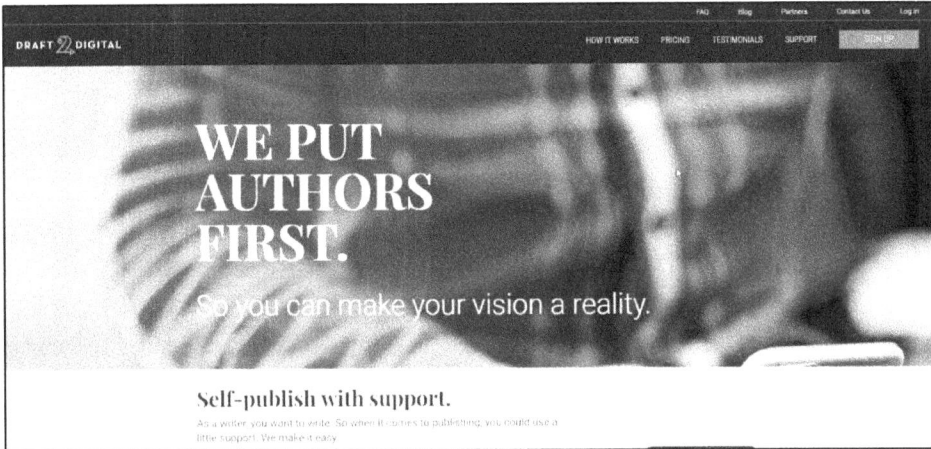

Many self-publishing companies distribute through these platforms, such as Lulu and BookBaby, which will set up your print book and format your e-book for sale on Kindle. You can variously pay for design and production work and earn money back through varying royalty deals, while the platforms are free when you set up book publishing with them directly.

However, while you can publish on multiple platforms, different companies have different formatting requirements for submitting your material. For example, Smashwords has very specific requirements for formatting your Word document, so you have to set the size of the fonts, spacing, use of tabs, lines between chapters, and other requirements according to specs, which can take a long time for formatting. For example, it took about 5 or 6 hours for one of my assistants to format a 200 to 300 page manuscript. By contrast, Draft2Digital has software that can do all of the necessary set up from a Word document, and Kindle can convert a Word file or PDF into its own format.

While you can set up a Kindle account directly, if you publish your book on CreateSpace, which I recommend, you can easily convert your published book there to Kindle. In fact, all you have to do after your CreateSpace book is approved is to click the "Publish on Kindle" button and create an account there, with your name, contact information, credit card, and tax information, just as on CreateSpace. After that, you can import your already created CreateSpace cover, and you can have Kindle convert your already CreateSpace PDF or upload another interior file as a Word or PDF document. Usually, I have found that the CreateSpace interior files convert to Kindle's platform just fine, including closing up spaces between chapters and eliminating extra pages. But if you want even more control of the process, create a separate Word document without any blank pages and spaces between chapters.

**Publishing Your Book on Kindle**

Following is an example of what the Kindle interface looks like after you click the "Publish on Kindle" button. Once you provide the necessary account information and transfer your files from CreateSpace or upload your own files, you have to set up distribution and pricing.

As indicated below, the cover for one of my books *Turn Your Video or PowerPoint into a PDF or Book* is already set up to be transferred to Kindle if I want. I can also download the cover and interior file onto my computer for future use. This process is especially useful if you have previously uploaded a Word file, since now you have a PDF, too.

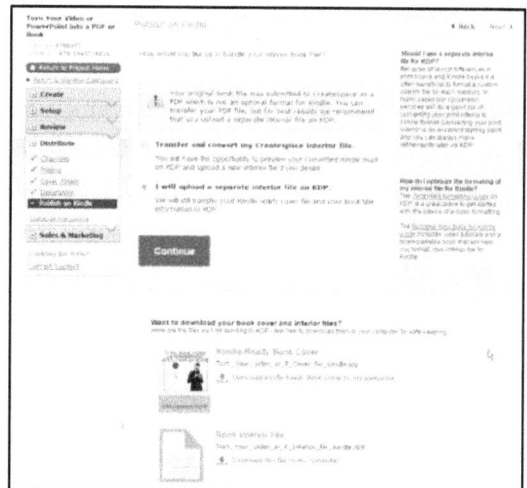

Thus, you can opt to transfer your CreateSpace file to Kindle or upload a file from your computer. You can also download the cover file created in CreateSpace onto your computer to use yourself for other purposes. If you are uploading a file from your computer, Kindle prefers using a doc, docx, HTML, MOBI, ePub, RTF, Plain Text, and KPF (Kindle Package File), but it will accept PDF files.

Then you indicate if this is a public domain work or not (it isn't), and if you want to select digital rights management (DRM), or not. Choosing DRM means you won't permit the unauthorized transfer of your

Kindle book to others. If you are mainly using your book for promotion, you don't want this limitation. But if primarily hope to earn money from your book, you would designate that you want the DRM rights.

Once you submit your files to Kindle (or KDP, short for Kindle Direct Publishing), you sign in with your account if you have already set this up. Or you can sign up for an account now.

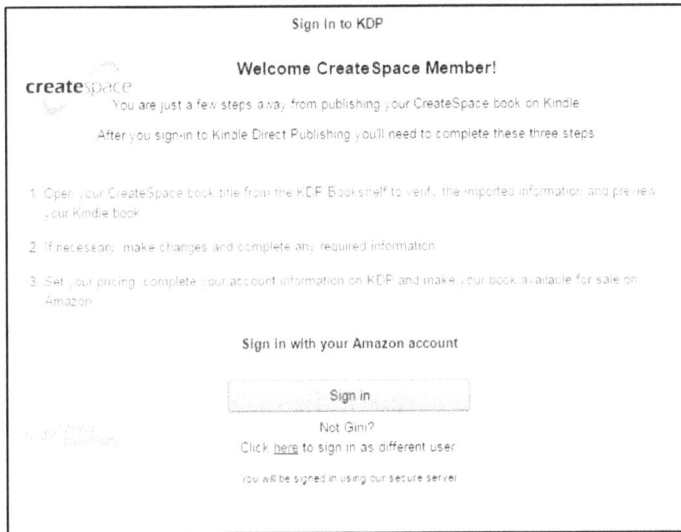

After you sign in or sign up, your book will be added to your KDP bookshelf, and you can make changes or add to the information about your book. You can see a preview of how it will look on a smartphone.

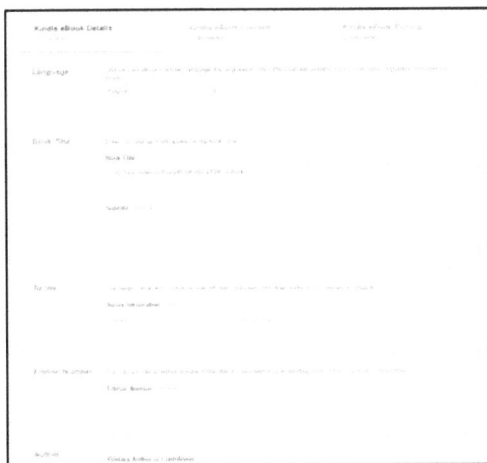

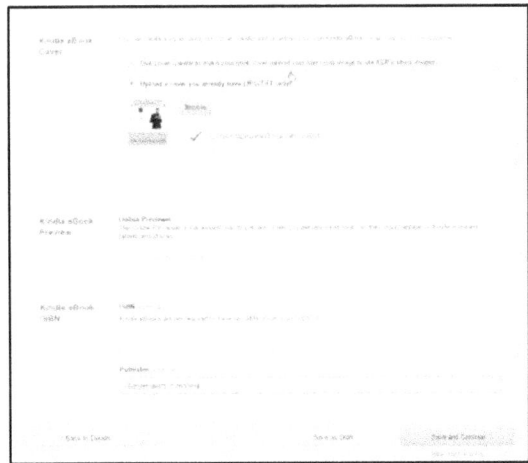

Finally, you set up your distribution and pricing arrangements. If you want, you can enroll in KDP select, which is an exclusive arrangement in which Kindle promotes your book for three months, in return for your sharing the royalty fund with other books in the program. The royalty amount is based on how many pages people read of your book, and during this time, your book is only on Kindle. To end your book in KDP Select, you have to cancel, or the 90 day period automatically renews. Since you want to make your e-book available through other distribution sources, don't enroll in KDP select.

Normally you want to select all territories. You can choose between receiving a royalty of 35-70%. If you are mainly using the book for promotion, a 35% royalty is fine, since you can price it between $0-$200, though generally it's best to make it free or sell it for $.99 or $1.99. To get a higher royalty with a higher profit return, you can get a 70% royalty by pricing your book between $2.99 and $9.99. To help you decide, you can see the amount of royalty you would get at each price point and royalty rate for each sale in the countries where Kindle books are distributed.

Another option is whether you want to include your book in Kindle's Matchbook program, whereby anyone who buys a print book from Amazon can buy the Kindle edition for a reduced price. This ranges from free to $2.99, with the available price points depending on your how you have set your Kindle price. For example, since I set the price at $2.99, my only options were $.99 or free. You additionally can include your book in Kindle's lending program or not, though you have to do this if you choose the 70% royalty. This lending program means that buyers can lend a book they have purchased on Amazon to friends and family members for up to 14 days. If your book is designed for promotional purposes, set it to free.

Then, you are done and ready to publish. Just click the "Publish Your Kindle Book" button and you're ready to go.

You will get an acknowledgment that your book will be available on Kindle within 72 hours. If you have not already published your book on CreateSpace, you can use the same information and manuscript to readily publish it there.

For example, here's the announcement I got to let me know my book would be up for sale on Amazon in the next 3 days.

# CHAPTER 14: CREATING AN AUDIOBOOK: PUBLISHING WITH ACX/AUDIBLE

Given the popularity of audiobooks, these are produced by numerous publishers, including large traditional publishers who are producing audio versions of hardcover and paperback books. A growing number of publishers and online retailers are selling these books directly to consumers too. Some of the most well-known ones include Kindle Unlimited, Scribd, Barnes and Noble, iTunes, Audiobooks.com, Apple iBooks, and Audible.

The royalty rates are very favorable to audiobook authors. On most platforms, including Audible, iTunes, and Amazon, authors receive an average of 25% to 35% of the retail price.

**Recording Standards**

While authors can create their own audiobooks by recording their books or manuscripts, they have to meet minimum standards to produce a recording that is acceptable to audiobook distributors and retailers. You can't just connect a mic to a mixing board, because you have to control for all sorts of things for a professional quality recording. Among other things, you have to have consistency in your audio levels, room tone, noise level, spacing, and pronunciation. Keeping a consistent sound level is especially important, because if there are extreme highs and lows in volume, the listener has to keep adjusting the volume or the receiver, which detracts from the listening experience and may result in poor reviews and reduced sales, as Michael Kozlowski notes in "Global Audiobook Trends and Statistics for 2016."[1]

Some other requirements include these:

- You need to include opening and closing credits which state the title of the book, the name of the author, or authors, and the publisher.

- You need to state that this is "the end" at the conclusion.

- You must have a 1 to 5 minute sample, so the prospective listener can get an idea of the rest of the book in order to make a purchase decision.

- You must record your book in separate chapter by chapter segments for many distributors, such as Audible, Apple, and Amazon. You can't just record a single file that is several hours long.

- You have to include .5 to 1 second of room tone at the beginning and end of the recording.

[1]Michael Kozlowski, "Global Audiobook Trends and Statistics for 2016." http://goodreader.com/blog/interviews/global-audiobook-trends-and-statistics-for-2016

- You can't have any extraneous sounds, such as mic pops, mouse clicks, bursts of air, and street noises.
- You have to set the volume level to stay within a certain range.
- The uploaded file size can't be larger than a certain amount -- 170MB, and you have to record at a certain kilohertz (kHz) bandwidth – 44.1.

To achieve these requirements, you need professional quality recording equipment and a well-insulated, quiet area to make the recording. If you can't meet these standards, seek out a professional who is familiar with these requirements and has the necessary recording facilities.


**Recording and Marketing Your Audiobook**

One way to market your audiobook once you have a completed recording is through the Author's Republic (www.authorsrepublic.com). This distribution service was developed by Audiobooks.com, which provides a way to distribute independently published audiobooks to over a dozen audiobook retailers, including Audiobooks.com, Audible, iTunes, Amazon, Barnes & Noble, Scribd, Downpour, and Tunein. The company also distributes to libraries, such as through Findaway and Overdrive. Since the Author's Republic is an aggregate distributor, you have to already have a completed audiobook.

After you indicate which retailer and distributor partners you want to sell your audiobook, which could be all of them, you have to submit your book for a review. It has to meet the minimum standards. If not, the company will advise you accordingly so you can fix your files or metadata. Once your book passes muster, it can go on sale anywhere from 5 to 60 days after acceptance. After that, you will receive 70% of what your audiobook earns across over 30 channels, including all major distributors.

Should you need help in creating the audiobook, Author's Republic has a half-dozen recommendations for services that will create the book to professional standards, including Deyan Audio (www.deyanaudio.com), Spoke Media (www.spokemedia.com), Pro Audio Voices (www.proaudiovoices.com), VoicesforBooks.com (www.voicesforbooks.ccom), BeeAudio (www.beeaudio.com), e-AudioProductions (www.e-audioproductions.com), and Common Mode, Inc. (www.common-mode.com).

These services have all have worked closely with voice artists who can do your narration, though you can hire a union or non-union voice actor, such as through Voices.com (www.voices.com); Voice123 (www.voice123.com), or VoiceBunny (www.voicebunny.com). To find an actor, you post your job on their marketplace or review their talent pool to find the perfect narrator, based on a variety of options, including age, gender, and years of experience. These services can provide you with a pool of thousands of voice actors to choose from. A good way to choose among them is to provide a few paragraphs to a page of text from your manuscript for each actor to read from, along with some guidelines on what you are looking for in a narrator. Then, you can listen to a sample audition recording to help you decide.

In selecting a narrator, it is important to learn if they will take care of proofing, editing, and mastering the narration. While many narrators include these services, in order to provide you with a final recording that is ready to submit to distributors, some don't. This mastering involves preparing and transferring the recorded audio from the final mix to a data storage device. It is best if the narrator can handle this procedure rather than you having to find an audio engineer and editor. While there are experts in this area, such as SoundBetter (https://soundbetter.com) and e-AudioProductions (http://www.e-audioproductions.com), finding an outside editor and engineer can add another layer of complexity to getting a ready-to-market audiobook.

There are two major arrangements for paying for the narrator.

- Pay-for-Production, where you pay the narrator a set fee per finished hour of the recorded or fully-mastered produced audio. In this case, you own the recording, and can use it for as long and for whatever purpose you want.

- Royalty Share, where you split the revenue with the narrator, so the narrator receives a certain percentage of future sales. Usually this is a 50-50 split, but the narrator's percentage can vary depending on his or her experience and visibility in the industry.

If you are paying the narrator, the cost of a finished audiobook can vary based on your book's length and the narrator's charge per finished hour of audio. Generally, each hour of recorded audio takes double that amount of time in the studio, so 5 recorded hours takes around 10 hours in the studio. Editing and other post-production work can be even longer, depending on the narrator's audio engineering skills.

To figure out the length of a narrated book, use the typical rate of speech of about 9400 words per hour and divide this into the number of words in your book. So if your book has 30,000 words, this will be a little over 3 hours to narrate. Then, factor in the cost per hour of the narrator. If a narrator is a SAG or AFTRA union member, the minimum fee per finished hour is $225; while non-union professions are free to charge whatever they want, which is commonly $100 to $250 per hour. So for a 3 hour narrated book, the cost would be about $300 to $750.

Alternatively, if you can find a narrator who likes your book and would like to narrate it for a royalty split, that can be more cost effective. This royalty split is ideal if you have many books to turn into audiobooks, since you won't know how well the books are doing until they are in distribution and you launch a marketing campaign to boost sales. That's what I've done with my audiobooks – 40 so far with sales of about 525 units in five months. While one book has sold nearly 200 copies, most have sold around 10 to 30 copies at an average price of $4 for the shorter books up to $8 for the longer books. If you do the math, you'll find that it was much more cost effective to share the royalties than to pay a narrator.

For example, the book that sold 200 copies earned about $1600, with $800 to me. But if I hired a narrator for this book of about 90,000 words, I would have paid about $1000 to $2500 for 10 hours of recording. And my costs relative to earnings would have been much more in the case of my other books, which sold 10 to 30 copies. Plus since I had 40 books, my costs would have been astronomical. So definitely, if you can set up a shared royalty deal, do so, unless you are certain you can sell a ton of books and earn over $1000, so you net more than you would with a royalty share arrangement.

Certainly, you can narrate your book yourself, though then you need the appropriate equipment, including a computer or tablet with recording software, a good microphone, and headphones for self-monitoring, as well as a quiet location. Additionally, you need a good voice for the narration, and you have to follow the appropriate procedures for making the recording, editing it, and handling the post-production. Whew!

**Using the ACX-Audible Platform to Record and Sell Your Book**

If these arrangements to find a narrator or narrate your book yourself sound complicated, that's because they are. The easy solution, which I have done, is using the ACX platform that connects book authors to narrators and distributes the books through Audible, which has been the dominant audiobook self-publishing company for a number of years. ACX is a division of Audible.com, which is an Amazon subsidiary.

This platform provides an easy-to-use format, which enables you to select your printed book on Amazon and offer it, within minutes, to hundreds if not thousands of narrators on a royalty share arrangement – or you can offer to pay the narrator if you prefer.

If a narrator is interested in narrating your book, he or she submits a short audition, and you can choose among those auditioning who will be the best fit. If the narrator accepts your offer, you are on. You send the full manuscript; then the narrator sends you the first 15 minutes. If you approve this, the narrator completes the book. If you approve this final narration, the ACX team reviews the files to make sure they are up to standards. If they are, your audiobook will be up for sale on Audible in about two weeks. Or the ACX team will tell you and the narrator if there are any problems, and what to do to fix them. Once the narrator makes the fix, you submit the files for approval once again. Meanwhile, you have to provide the artwork for the cover, using either original art, or you can adapt the original book cover to fit. After that, Audible seeks to market and sell your book, including on Amazon, and iTunes, as well as on Audible. You can supplement these efforts with your own promotional campaign, along with an email outreach to your mailing list and leads.

## How You Can Use ACX

To show how the ACX platform works, here are step-by-step guidelines so you know what to expect and can prepare your materials to use this system.

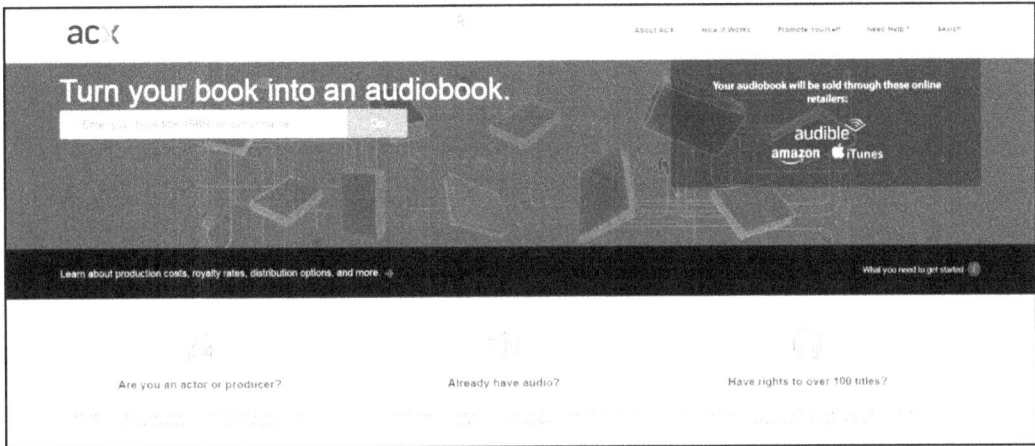

As with any platform, the first step is to set up an account.

Then, you add a title that is already on Amazon, confirm that you have the audio rights for your book so you are the rights holder. Next, you create a profile for your title by describing your book and the type of narrator best suited for it, such as a speaker who is authoritative, inspirational, motivational, warm, or has other characteristics, and is male, female, or either. Then post a 1-2 page excerpt from your book as an audition script for potential narrators.

Next, you offer your book to narrators to produce your book. Those who are interested in being considered will send you auditions, and you listen to them. After that you make your choice. In all but two postings for narrators, I found I got at least one, and sometimes two, three or four interested narrators.

Once you choose the narrator you like most, you make an offer for a royalty share or payment deal based on the narrator/producer completing the first 15 minutes by a certain date, and completing the whole audiobook by a future date. I have only used the royalty share arrangement, and each time my offer has been accepted, with one exception, the narrator/producer has completed the book, though sometimes a little later than originally agreed. In the one case that the narrator didn't come through, I offered up the project again and found another narrator who completed the book.

After you approve the first 15 minutes, the narrator will record he full project. If you want the narrator to make any corrections, you can do so and you can ask for up to two rounds of corrections, though I have only made a few minor corrections, such as asking the narrator to shorten the copyright notice or move the author's bio to the end.

Once the book is done, you submit it to ACX to review. If you have agreed to pay the producer, you pay the producer directly once you approve it, and you now have a non-exclusive arrangement with ACX and Audible, so you can distribute the book through other channels. Alternatively, ACX treats any shared royalty agreement as an exclusive arrangement. Once your book passes the review process, it goes up for sale.

Now you can promote the book in various ways, and ACX offers a variety of suggestions, including using email marketing and the social media. As the book sells, you will earn royalties, payable each month, paid directly into your bank, and you can see how your book is doing on your sales dashboard.

So that's a brief overview of how the recording-sales process works. Now I'll illustrate this with some examples, showing how I posted and worked out arrangements with a narrator for one of my books.


## An Example of Using the ACX Platform

As the following illustrates, ACX offers three options when you sign up and want to turn your book into an audiobook to be sold on Audible. One is the royalty share arrangement where you split the 40% royalty with the narrator. Another is where you pay the narrator a flat fee for production and agree to an exclusive option with Audible in return for receiving the full 40% yourself. Finally you have the option of paying for production and having a non-exclusive arrangement with Audible, so you can arrange for distribution with other parties in return for a 25% royalty with Audible.

## Three Options For You

Here's a summary comparison of the three basic payment and distribution options currently available for audio production deals on ACX. Note that this is a summary only. See the ACX Book Posting Agreement and Production Standard Terms for actual terms that apply.

| | OPTION 1 Royalty Share with Exclusive Distribution to Audible | OPTION 2* Pay For Production (Flat Fee) with Exclusive Distribution to Audible | OPTION 3* Pay For Production (Flat Fee) with Non-Exclusive Distribution Rights to Audible |
|---|---|---|---|
| **Payment to Producer** Choose a Royalty Share deal or a one-time Pay for Production fee | Royalty payments from Audible are shared equally between Rights Holder and Producer | Rights Holder pays Producer a one-time fee for production | |
| **Distribution** Grant Audible exclusive or non-exclusive distribution rights. Either way is powerful— our third party distributors get audiobooks in front of buyers. **The difference is this:** Royalty rates are higher when distribution is left exclusively to ACX. | ACX exclusive distribution— through Audible, Amazon, and iTunes** via ACX, as well as wherever else Audible chooses. Under this model, Audible has the exclusive right to distribute the audiobook. If you choose this option, the audiobook cannot be distributed by any entity except ACX **in any market or format.** | ACX exclusive distribution— through Audible, Amazon, and iTunes** via ACX, as well as wherever else Audible chooses. Under this model, Audible has the exclusive right to distribute the audiobook. If you choose this option, the audiobook cannot be distributed by any entity except ACX **in any market or format.** | Non-exclusive distribution— through Audible, Amazon, and iTunes** via ACX, as well as wherever else Rights Holder chooses. Under this model, Rights Holder can grant distribution rights to parties other than Audible **in any market or any format** |
| **Royalty Rate** | **40% of retail sales split equally** between Rights Holder and Producer. In other words, each gets 20% of total retail sales. | **40% of retail sales paid to** Rights Holder. | **25% of retail sales paid to** Rights Holder. |
| **Bounty Payment** Earnings can increase with these extra payments. | ACX pays Rights Holder and Producer $50 every time the audiobook is the first audiobook purchased by an AudibleListener™ member on Audible. The $50 payment is split 50-50 between Rights Holder and Producer, amounting to $25 each. See terms. | ACX pays Rights Holder $50 every time the audiobook is among the first audiobook purchased by an AudibleListener™ member on Audible. See terms. | |
| **Royalty Payment Frequency** ACX sends a monthly statement and a check or electronic payment to US users(when there's at least $50 to be paid). Users in the UK receive electronic payments and statements monthly. | Separate payments sent to Rights Holder and to Producer (when there's at least $50 to be paid). | Payments to Rights Holder (when there's at least $50 to be paid). | |

To turn your book into an audiobook, click "Add Your Title" and enter the name of your book which has already been published on Amazon in the search bar, and it will turn up. If other books have the same or a very similar title, they will show up, too. Once you find your book, click the "This is My Book" button. If you have multiple versions, such as one book in color, another with black and white photos, or books in different sizes, select one of them, since the narration will be the same.

Since this is an audiobook, the illustrations normally won't matter, unless they are an essential part of the book. In that case, once the final audiobook is approved, you will send the ACX staff a PDF with the illustrations, along with instructions so the reader can follow along.  Or the narrator may need to add in some instructions in the text to refer to a particular illustration.  Otherwise, figure that the illustrations won't be included in the audiobook.

Where there are multiple versions, pick the book with the best cover. For example, choose the cover that doesn't include any special language about which edition this is, such if a cover indicates this is the pocket edition or has full color or black and white photos.

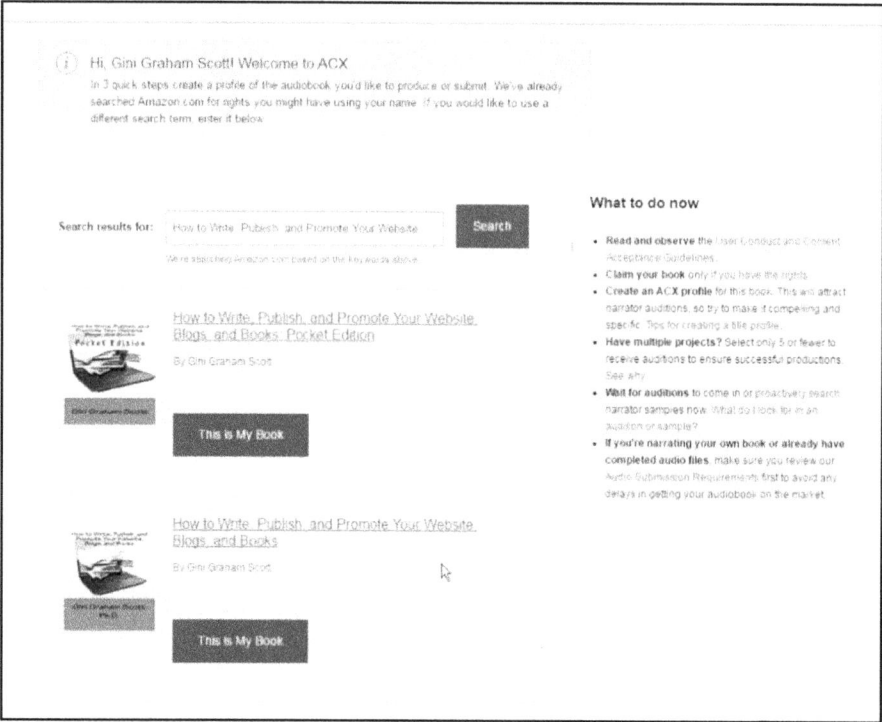

Next, unless you plan to provide the audio files yourself, indicate that you are looking for a narrator and producer.  Choose this option, unless you know what you are doing in creating an audio recording or want to work with your own experienced narrator, because the specs for creating an audiobook are really demanding and you can't readily do this without the right equipment and knowledge.

## How can ACX work for you:

Whether you want to find a Producer to help you create your audiobook, or if you already have the audio, ACX is here for you.

Simply choose the path to the right that best fits your needs and get started.

I'm looking for someone to narrate and produce my audiobook.

I already have audio files for this book, and I want to sell it.

I want to find out how to narrate this book and upload files later.

The next step is agreeing to ACX's terms, indicating that you understand this will be a binding agreement with the narrator/producer. You also agree that you have full audio rights and that you have the option to make this an exclusive or nonexclusive deal.

These are our terms. Please read and agree to continue...

Print

Legal Contracts

### ACX Book Posting Agreement

**Last revised 04/06/2014**

**Version 2.0**

This **ACX Book Posting Agreement** ("Agreement") is a binding agreement between you, or the company or entity you represent, if you are entering into this Agreement on behalf of a company or entity ("you"), and Audible, Inc. ("Audible", "we" or "us"). It sets forth the terms you agree to when you make a book available for production as an audiobook on the audiobook production service and rights marketplace available at www.acx.com ("ACX") (any book you make available on ACX for production as an audiobook, a "Book"). You enter into this Agreement each time you make a Book available on ACX. That means that there is a separate Agreement between you and us for each Book you make available on ACX.

Clicking "Agree & Continue" will mean that:
- You have the audio rights to the book
- You want to add your book to ACX to get it produced as an audiobook.
- You will be able to meet potential narrators and producers for your book on ACX, and also may be contacted by audiobook publishers who may want to purchase the audio right to your book (and then produce it off of the ACX system).
- You will distribute the completed audiobook, at minimum, through ACX's distribution channel (Amazon, Audible and iTunes).
- You will have the choice to distribute it on an exclusive or non-exclusive basis.
- Any information you put into your book's ACX title profile is accurate.

I have read the above ACX Book Posting Agreement and agree to its terms

Agree & Continue

For the next step, describe your book, indicate copyright details, the book's best category, the narrator's voice, and other characteristics. For example, I indicated below that I am the copyright holder for both the print and audio book, that the print version was copyrighted in 2016, and that this is a non-fiction business book.

How to Write, Publish, and Promote Your Website, Blogs, and Books

By Gini Graham Scott

Required

1 Create Title Profile

2 Distribution

3 Review & Post

**About my book:**

HOW TO WRITE, PUBLISH, AND PROMOTE YOUR WEBSITE, BLOGS, AND BOOKS introduces a company that can help you with all types of writing and publishing &ndash; from books and scripts to blogs and website copy.   The book features these topics:   - Writing, ghostwriting, and editing   - Guidelines for getting started   - Self-publishing your book   - Finding publishers and agents   - Promoting your book, business, or yourself   - Promoting your articles or blogs   - Promoting your products or services   - Using a video or SEO for promotion   - Consulting on writing, publishing, and promotion   - Consulting on increasing creativity and problem solving   - Speaking, workshops and seminars    Gini Graham Scott has published over 50 books with major publishers and over 40

(1047 characters remaining)

The text above has been pulled from your book's Amazon description page and will be used to describe your book on Audible and iTunes. Changes to this description will be included on Audible and iTunes, but will not be reflected on your Amazon description page. Click above to begin editing.

**Copyright Information:**

This information will be read within the credits of the audiobook and it will also display on our retail sites when the audiobook is on sale. This information is optional at this time, but you will need to provide it by the time you send the manuscript to the Producer.

Print Copyright Owner Name: | Gini Graham Scott

Print Copyright Year(s): | 2016

Audiobook Copyright Owner: | Gini Graham Scott

Note: This is initially an optional field, but will need to be provided by the time you approve the first 15 minutes of your production. The copyright information will be read by the Audiobook Producer in the credits section of the book.

**My Book is:**
- Fiction
- Nonfiction

**Best category for my book is:**
Business ▼

**Describe the ideal narrator's voice:**

Gender       Language       Accent

Next, I entered some details about the ideal narrator's voice, such as indicating that either gender is fine, that this is in English, that I'd like someone with a general American accent and an adult with an authoritative voice.  After that, I can add more details about what I'm looking for in a narrator.  Generally, I indicated that I'm looking for someone who can speak as if they are having a conversation with the listener.  Finally, I added an audition script.  This should be a few pages from the full manuscript, put into its own PDF, Word, or text file, and uploaded using the Browse button. I usually upload the PDF file, which I used to upload the book on Amazon.

## Additional comments:

Just speak as if you are having a conversation with the listener|

(1935 characters remaining)

Here's your chance to provide directions or advice to Producers who may audition for this book. It is also a good place to make your book as appealing as possible to ACX Producers. For example, you can include marketing information, selling points, best-seller status, awards, foreign language translations and reviews. Additionally, please include information about the Author's reach and fan-base (i.e. 5,000 followers on Twitter, 8,000 fans on Facebook).

## Audition script:

Provide an audition script, so Producers will be able to submit their best performances for your work. You may upload your audition script, or click the link to type it in the box below.

### How to Select A Strong Audition Script:

- Your audition script should total no more than 2-3 pages.
- Your Producer will voice all characters and scenes in your book. If your book has multiple lead characters and/or accents, make sure to feature them in your audition script.
- We recommend selecting multiple relevant scenes featuring these characters to make up your audition script.
- Include additional detail on characters/scenes in the in the Audition Script Notes section below.
- Read more about selecting a strong audition script on our blog.

Audition Script Notes

(2000 characters remaining)

Choose audition script file from your computer:

Browse

You can upload Word, PDF or TXT files.

If you have trouble uploading your file, you can input your audition script as text.

Save & Continue

Next indicate the number of pages and your payment arrangements, which in this case was about 5000 words and a royalty share, which has to be an exclusive agreement with a 40% royalty, through Amazon, ACX, and iTunes. So far, I have found a royalty share has been a good arrangement, since I've sold 525 copies in 5 months, with almost no promotion by me, though if I began doing this with the techniques described in this book, I'm sure the sales would be much more.

After listing this information about the pages and payment arrangements, I can review the offer and make any changes. If it's fine, I can now post it and request auditions.

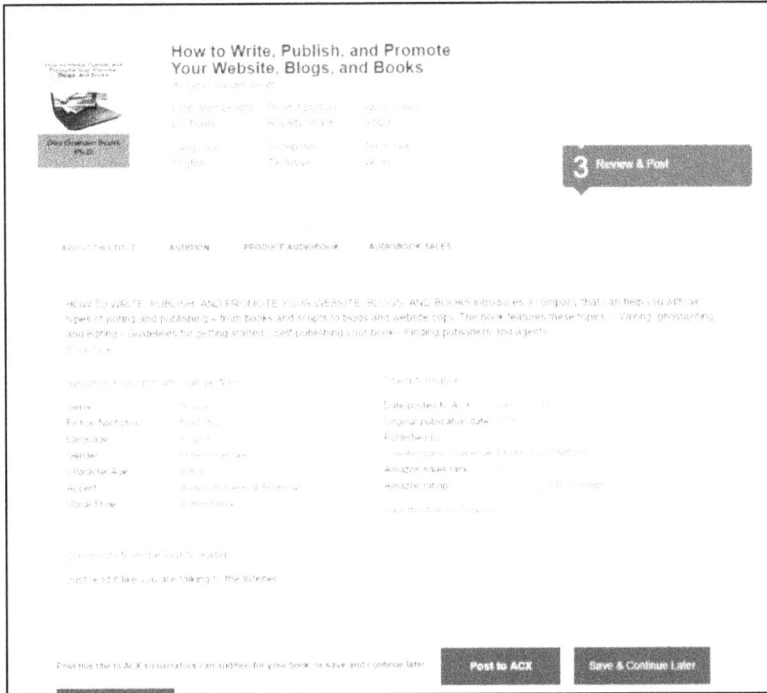

Once you click "Post to ACX," your book is available for auditions, along with any other books you have previously submitted. For instance, here's my book ready to go. The screen indicates any previous sales of other books as of that date, such as 509 sales in my own case.

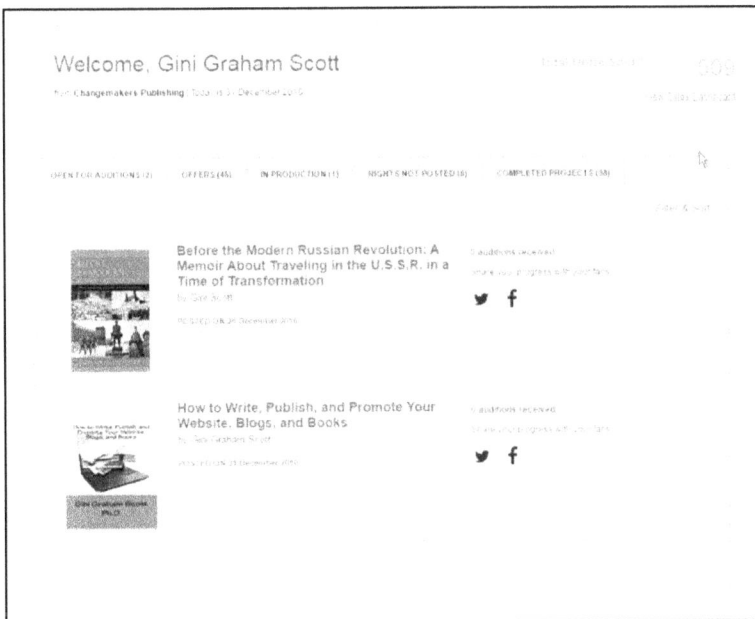

That whole process took about 10 minutes, so it is very quick to post a book and look for a narrator. Then, you wait for any auditions. If prospective narrators like your book, you will get a request, usually within a day or two of posting. In fact, within a day, I already got one audition, as indicated on the audition page below.

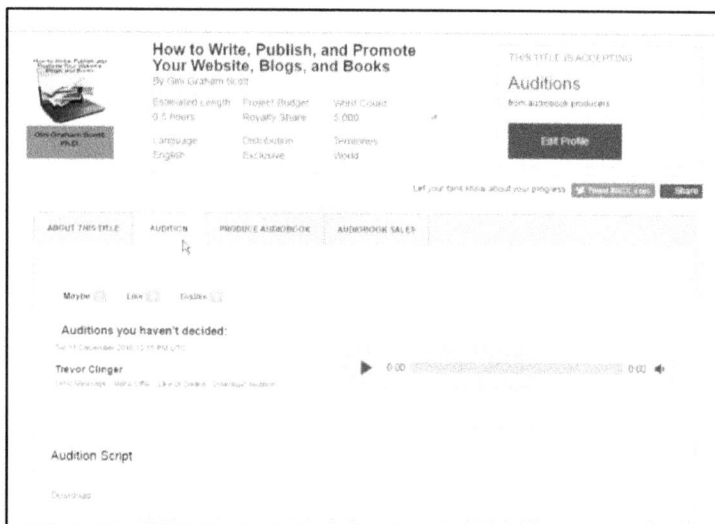

You then hear a short audio clip of a minute or two from each prospect, and you listen and decide who you prefer as a narrator. Once you decide, you make your royalty share offer and provide a date when you expect the first 15 minutes (I usually allow a week) and a date for the finished project (I usually allow 1 or 2 weeks, depending on the length of the book; a little longer if it's a longer book).

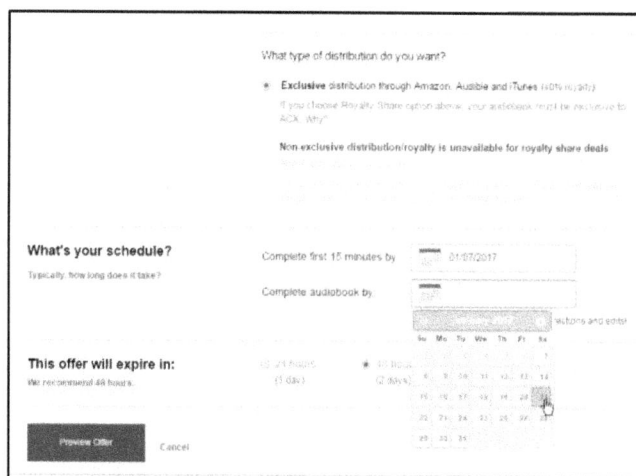

For example, here's my offer to one narrator below. After previewing my offer, if all looks okay, the offer goes to the narrator for his acceptance.

Should the prospective narrator need more time, he or she can write asking for an extension, though that has only happened to me twice out of 40 books.

After accepting the offer, the narrator will submit a 15 minute sample for your comments and any requested changes for your approval. If you ask for changes, the narrator will make them. Once you send your approval, the narrator will submit all of the files—one for the introduction with a title, author, and narrator; others for each chapter; an author's bio if you want one; and closing credits.

For example, the submission process looks something like this. After I have sent in my offer and the narrator has accepted it, I have to send the manuscript. Once I do, the narrator sends me the first 15 minutes. After I approve that, I wait for the finish audio, as in the case with my second manuscript *The Empowered Mind*.

**Welcome, Gini Graham Scott**

from Changemakers Publishing | Today is 1 January 2017

Total Units Sold

512

View Sales Dashboard

Along the way, the narrator will post files as they are completed, until they are finished, while I have to post a copy of the cover in at least a 2400 x 2400 pixel format. These steps are indicated below.

At each stage, you get to review and ask for any changes, and once you feel satisfied, you approve it. For example, here are the final files in my book project, along with my revised art, since my first artwork had large white borders on the sides rather than being a true square.

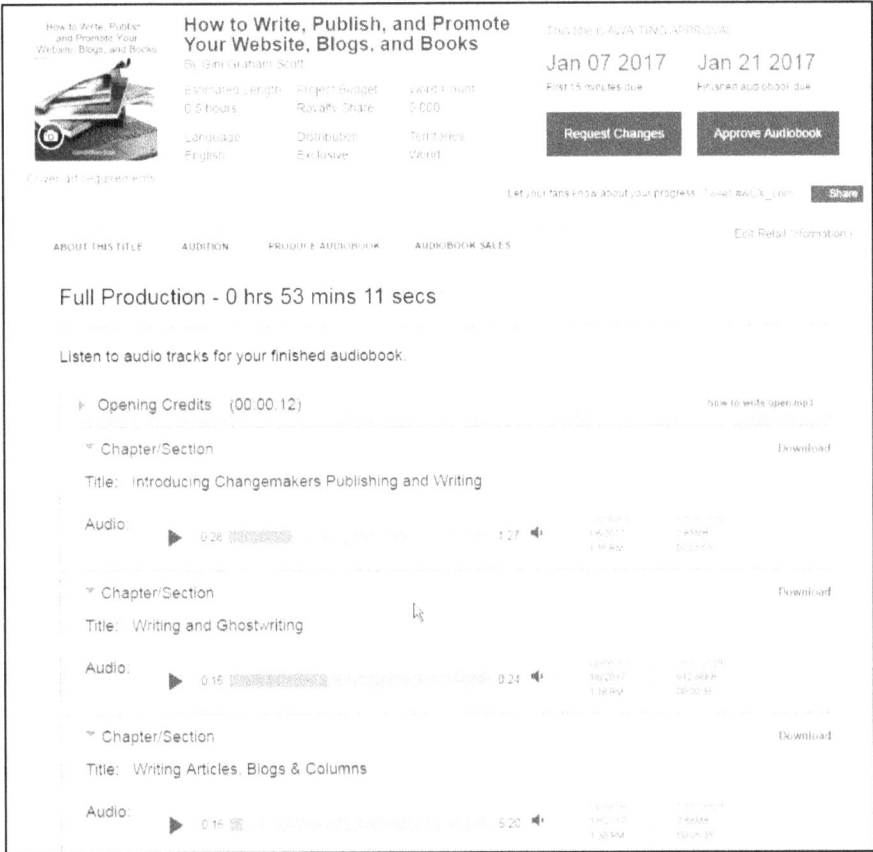

Once I approve the final recording with all the files, the ACX staff reviews it to see if the recording meets its audio standards. If any further changes are required, the ACX staff will advise the narrator and the author what to correct. My experience is that the narrators usually get it right the first time, and if necessary, quickly make any corrections.

Meanwhile, if you haven't already done so, you have to upload your cover art, which you can adapt from your CreateSpace or Kindle Cover, so it's in a square format of at least 2400 x 2400 pixels. You can't just slap on a border, unless the border fits in with the color and look of your original art, so you may have to do some PhotoShopping to crop or otherwise adjust your cover to ACX's specs.

Once both your cover and audiobook are approved, you are done. The book goes up on sale, generally within 2 weeks, and you will even get some complimentary download coupons you can pass on to friends, associates, and the media to help stimulate sales.

So as you can see, this is a fairly simple, easy to navigate way to quickly get your audiobook published, once you have a published POD or ebook on Amazon. If you don't find an outside narrator for a royalty share, you can always try to do it yourself or find a narrator and producer to create the finished files for your audiobook.

# CHAPTER 15: USING A PDF TO SELL ONLINE

Another alternative with very little upfront cost is to create a PDF for each book. You already have a PDF created for other platforms, so you can use that.

## Adding a Cover

The only thing left to add to your PDF is an illustrated cover page to go at the beginning of the document. This is different from the Title Page, which has the title, author's name, and possibly the company name and contact information.

If you have already created a book cover for another program, such as for CreateSpace or Kindle, you can use that. To do so, turn the cover image into a PDF, if it already isn't in that format. If you have a JPEG from that cover, such as a JPEG from a Kindle-ready file created by CreateSpace, you can use that. If you have JPEG with both the front and back cover, crop that so you have only the front cover file for your book using Photoshop or another photo editing program. Once you have your final JPEG or image for the cover, save that as a PDF. Then, insert that PDF file at the beginning of the PDF file for your book.

## Selling Your PDF from Your Website

You can sell your PDF directly from your website. To do so, feature it on your home page or set up a page for it. Include a photo of the cover and ad copy promoting your book. Emphasize the benefits and the main topics your book covers, and how this will help readers.

Include a buy button by your book so people can buy, either by paying through PayPal or a credit card. Then, include a link where buyers can download the PDF, along with a "thank you" for buying your book. If you have additional related books or other products and services, you can offer an upsell.

Typically, individuals selling from their website use two main delivery platforms for processing payments and delivering the PDF. These are aWeber and GetResponse. A link to their websites is featured below. For more details visit their websites.

## AWeber

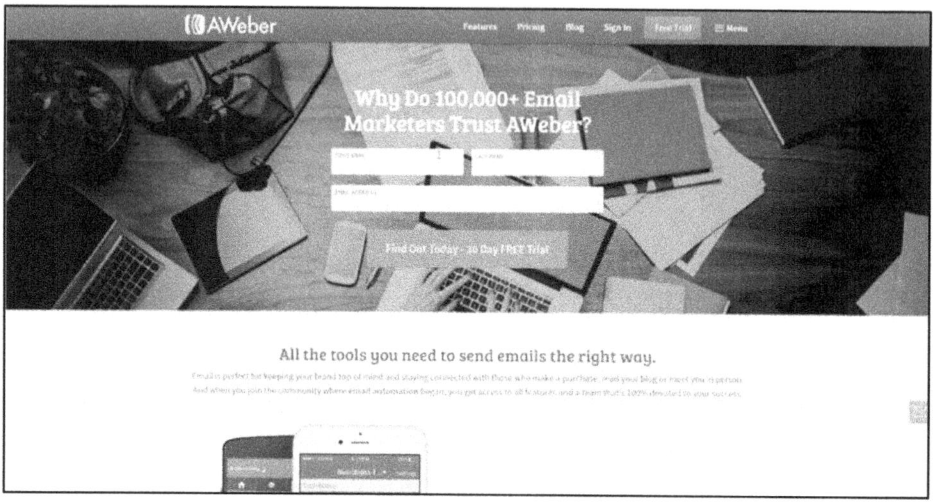
AWeber
Why Do 100,000+ Email Marketers Trust AWeber?
All the tools you need to send emails the right way.

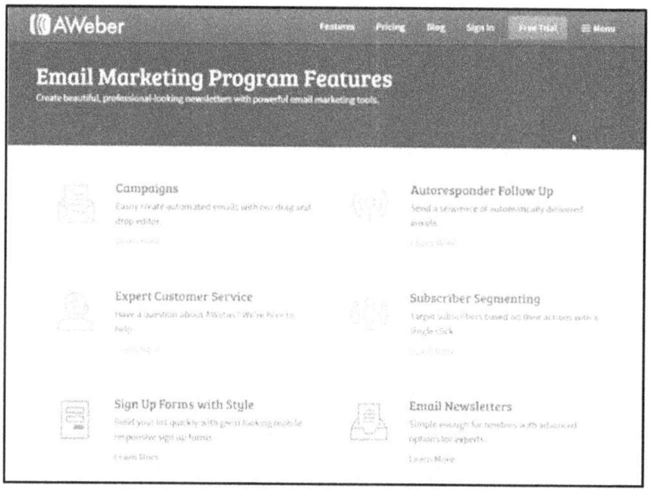
AWeber
Email Marketing Program Features
Create beautiful, professional-looking newsletters with powerful email marketing tools.
Campaigns
Autoresponder Follow Up
Expert Customer Service
Subscriber Segmenting
Sign Up Forms with Style
Email Newsletters

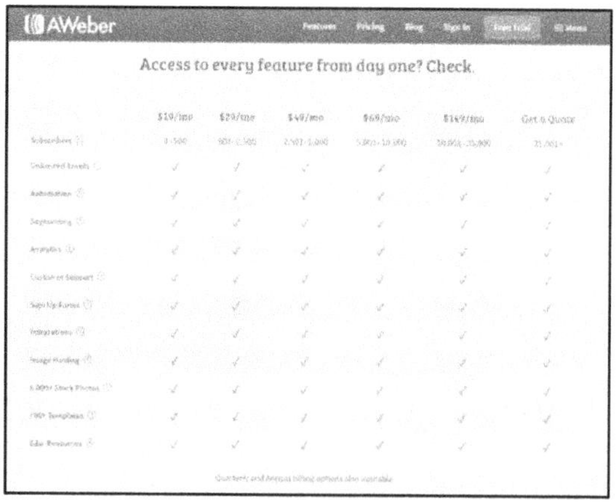
AWeber
Access to every feature from day one? Check.

# Get Response

## Setting Up an Online Digital Sales Platform

Besides from selling from your website, you can sell on sales platforms, which have a network of affiliates who can sell your book in return for a commission. Commonly, commissions are from 50-75%, which may sound high, but you have virtually no costs for a PDF, so it's worth the high commission, because marketing is the hard part. Many affiliates have already developed their own email lists and will offer your product to them. You can also become an affiliate to market others' products. Potential customers come to these sales platforms seeking books, as well as products in a number of categories.

Generally, these platforms are best for books in the self-help, success in business, and how-to categories. So if you have written a memoir, novel, or thoughtful book on social issues, this is probably not a good platform for you.

You can sell books by themselves on these platforms, though typically they are combined with a video where you introduce the PDF, and commonly, these PDFs of books or chapters from a book are combined with video modules to create an online course, as described in the next chapter.

You generally need some sales materials to go along with your book, and some platforms have classes on how to develop your materials and set up your book or product for sale. For example, ClickBank has ClickBank University for training and ClickBank Builder to help you create the various components for creating a course and your sales materials. Click Funnels has its own software to help you create these materials to sell your products.

Commonly, when you sell a book or other products through these platforms, you have to develop a sales funnel starting with your pitch page, where you give a brief video pitch on how your book will benefit a reader. Online marketers call these video pitches "VSLs," which refers to a video sales letter. If customers are interested, they can buy whatever is offered on that page. If they buy and pay, usually with a credit card or PayPal, they are directed to a Thank You page, which thanks them for their order and indicates what to do to access it, such as directing the customer to click on a link to download the PDF. Or the Thank You page directs them to another page with that download link.

In addition, you can develop some sales materials, such as advertising banners or ad copy, to attract affiliates to sell your book.

The companies with these platforms offer extensive information on how to create a great promotional campaign for your book or product, which you can review if you are interested in this type of selling. Here the links for the most popular sales platforms – ClickBank, Click Funnels, and ZVZoo.

## ClickBank (www.clickbank.com)

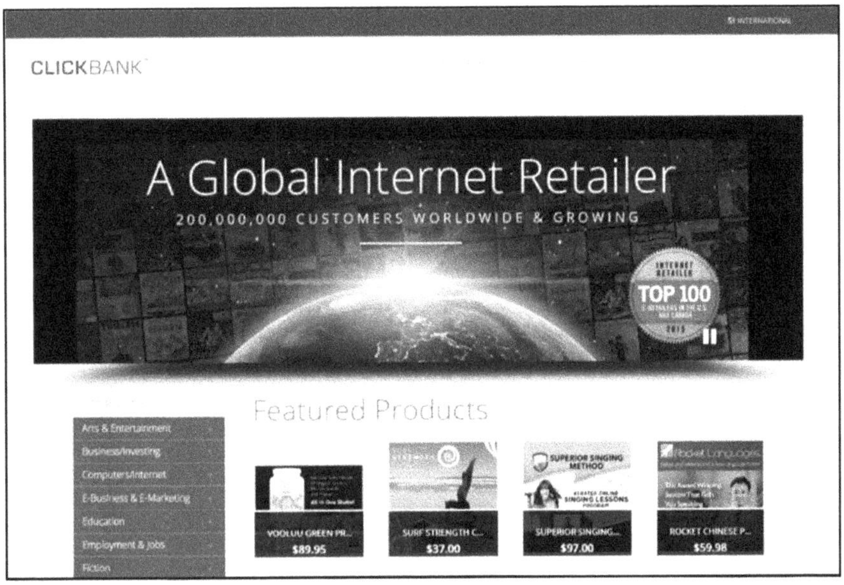


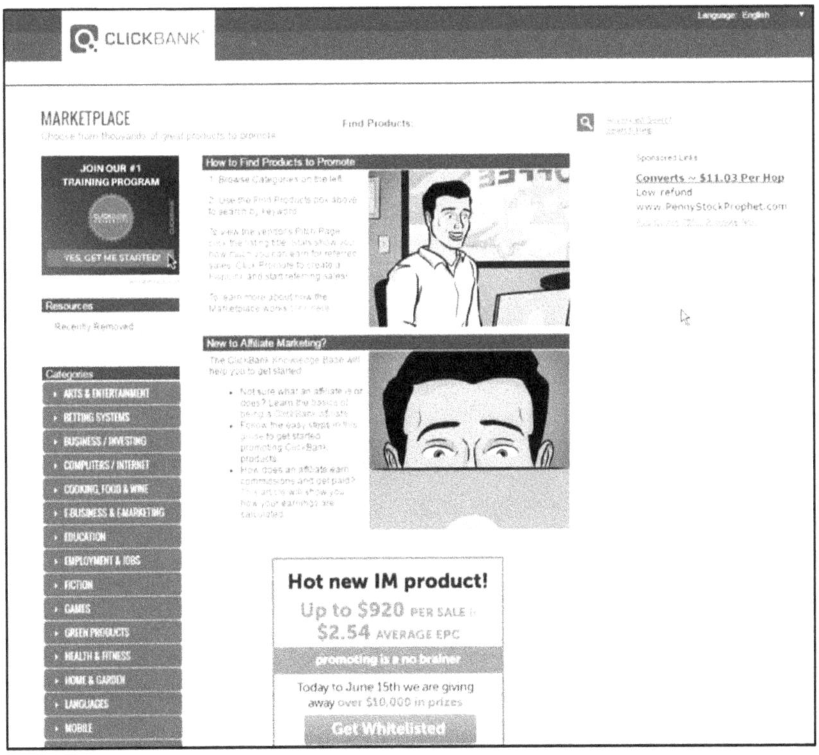

**Click Funnels (www.clickfunnels.com)**

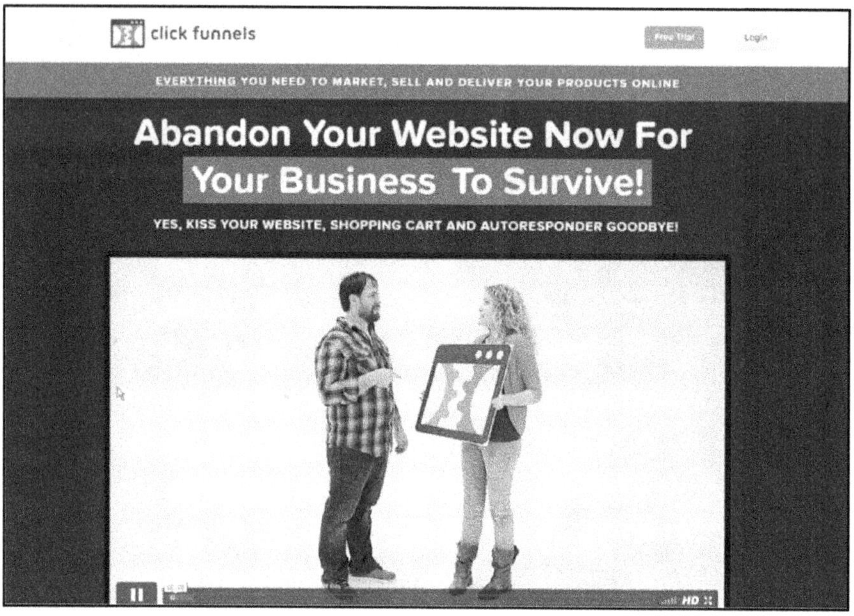


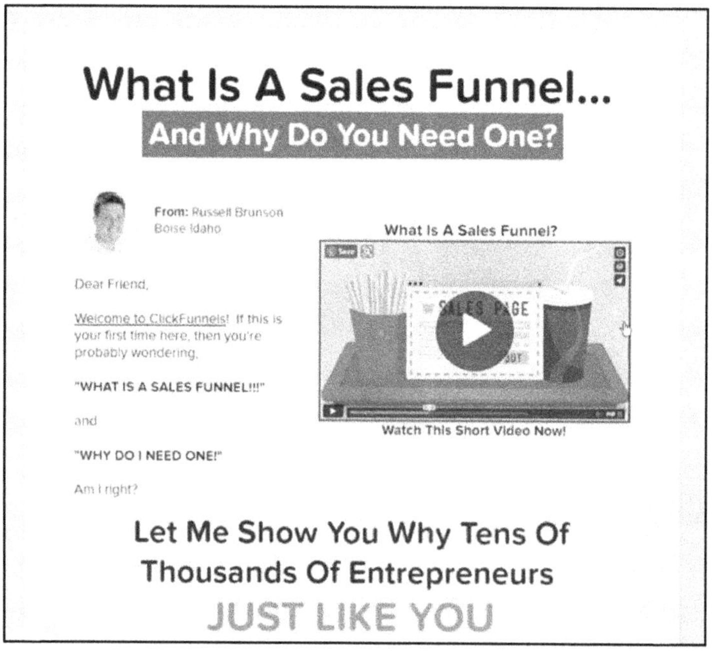

## JVZoo (www.zvzoo.com)

The global technology that drives online sales

# Everything you need to Succeed

It's easy and FREE to be a Seller or Affiliate on JVZoo! One account allows you to be a Seller, an Affiliate or both. JVZoo offers powerful, easy to use, industry-leading features all in one place that empower all of our users to connect and succeed online.

## Sell on JVZoo

Sellers can create unlimited buy buttons and add as many products or webinars as desired to our Product Library and never be charged a fee.

## Become a JVZoo Affiliate

Affiliates have instant access to all of our affiliate tools and training. Sign up to start earning instantly paid commissions today.

**Instant and Delayed Affiliate Payments**
Give your affiliates instant or delayed payments while keeping control of refunds.

**Stylish Button Creation**
Choose from a variety of pre-tested buy buttons. Instantly create dime sales that boost sales with.

**Digital Delivery and Protection**
JVZoo customer portal will instantly deliver your products for you, saving you time and money.

**Free to Join and Promote Products**
Sign up and gain instant access to JVZoo's Product Library to find the perfect products to promote to your audiences.

**Earn up to 100% Instant Commissions**
Promote products via your blog, email list, website, PPC, etc. Commissions are paid to you from the vendors directly to your PayPal.

**Searchable Affiliate Product Library**
Up-to-date conversion and EPC details let you know what to expect from a promotion with network-wide vendors available.

It takes some extra work to market your book through one of these platforms, and I recommend signing up for the company's classes or builder programs on how to set up your system. There may be a substantial expense to sign up for these programs – about $500-1500, but the cost can be worth it if you are serious about marketing your book, and particularly if you have a series of books. With the right product, sales can be very substantial. Some marketing people with the right product have generated thousands of sales each day with the help of their affiliates, so they are making thousands of dollars each week, and sometimes that much in a day.

Thus, there is plenty of potential for book sales through these platforms, and you have minimal costs for creating the PDF file to sell your book.

# CHAPTER 16: CREATING A COURSE: USING POWERPOINTS AND VIDEOS

Creating a video or video series can be a powerful way to promote your book, as well as a course you can sell. You can use a PowerPoint or series of PowerPoints to create these videos. I'll describe the process here briefly, and I will discuss this in more detail in a future book.

Depending on your preference, you can create a video with you talking against a professional-looking background or combine PowerPoint slides with a voiceovers by you. If you prefer to use slides for most of your sales video or course, start off with you talking briefly to introduce the rest of the video, since people want to first connect with you. Then, if you don't feel comfortable talking for the rest of the video or want to use photos and video clips to feature your book, use those and PowerPoint slides for most of your presentation.

Figure on 1 to 3 minutes for sales videos and 3 to 10 minutes, and sometimes up to 15 to 20 minutes, for the videos with content for your course.

Generally, in designing the videos for a course, feature the highlights of your book or each chapter in a series of videos. Provide a link so the viewer can download a PDF for each chapter or the whole book for more information.

## Creating Your Video`

Decide in advance the purpose of the video. It might be:
- a short 1-3 minute sales video, where you pitch your book or course to prospective customers,
- a short 3-10 minute introduction, featuring highlights of each chapter or the book as a whole, after which you invite viewers to download a more detailed PDF,
- a comprehensive video class, such as a single class of 40-90 minutes or a series of modules of about 5-15 minutes each.

You can also cut up the final video into a sales video, intro, and full class. You may be able to use pieces of the video to create a sales video. However, it is better to create the sales video separately if your style of presentation differs when you are providing informational content and seeking sales.

While you can bring in a professional to create your video, an inexpensive way to film this is to set up a tripod and talk directly to the viewer. You can have samples of your book or other products with you to show viewers, as well as have charts or a white board or blackboard to write on behind you. Alternatively, you can weave in clips of photos, PowerPoint slides, or short videos or your talk.

You can easily add in these inserts and do simple editing to more around or delete sections of your video. To do so, use an inexpensive video editing program, such as Camtasia.

To help you make an effective video, prepare a list of bulleted talking points in advance to guide you, so you know what to say. Additionally, practice your talk so you can present it smoothly. Another approach which some speakers use is writing a short talk; then you practice that. You don't have to memorize what you plan to say word for word, but writing out bullet points or your whole talk will help you become very familiar with the main points you want to make. Whatever method you use, the point is to create a talk that covers the highlights of your book.

As for the background, a simple professional looking background works well. Perhaps add a shelf or table-top display of your books. Preferably use an uncluttered background, though you might soften a plain wall by putting a plant in front of it.

It's best to film your video indoors in a quiet room, since you may experience background sounds outdoors.

If you have an assistant to help with the video camera, that's great. Or film your video yourself by using a tripod. Set up the camera or smartphone to take a horizontal shot, and use the viewer to position yourself for a waist-up medium shot. Finally, set the timer for a few seconds, so you can get back to where you are sitting, smile, and begin your talk.

**Creating Your PowerPoint and Turning It into a Video**

An alternate approach that works well is to begin with a short video where you personally introduce the rest of the video. Then, the video continues with a PowerPoint with a voiceover that you have turned into a video. You can create such a video presentation for each chapter or for the whole book.

Decide if you want your PowerPoint video to be an overview of the highlights of your book or course, or if this will be a longer video that presents the main content of your book. In either case, combine the video with a link to your more comprehensive presentation of your book in a PDF.

In creating these PowerPoints for each chapter or for the whole book, use bullet points with short phrases or sentences to feature the main points in your talk. Depending on your style, you can talk extemporaneously; using these highlights to trigger your memory for topics to cover, or you can follow along closely with the written content on each slide.

Once you have practiced what to say and are ready, add the voiceover to your PowerPoint presentation. To add this, you can use the "Add On" feature in PowerPoint 10 and up. Just click "Add On" and this will open up the online

Camtasia recording studio. If it's not already there, download the app to get it.

Then, as you go from slide to slide, talk as much as you want for each slide. To do this, start talking about the slide using the mic on your computer, and when you are done with the content on each slide, click to go to the next. Keep doing this until you get to the end of the PowerPoint, and the program will ask you if that's the last slide. To indicate that it is, click that you are finished. Then, save your PowerPoint with your voiceover as a video.

While you can save your PowerPoint video without your voice and record your comments later, you can't control how long each PowerPoint slide stays on the screen. So normally, record your voiceover on your PowerPoint first, since you can adjust the timing for each slide, based on how much you want to say about it before moving on to the next slide.

At the end of the video, you can mention if your book is available as a download, or you can indicate this with some copy next to or under the video, or do both. The idea is to let people know where to click or what to do in order to get your chapters or whole book in a PDF.


**Promoting Your Course or Video**

Once you complete your video or course, the next step is promoting it – whether you are selling the video or series of videos individually or as part of a package with your PDF. While you can sell any PDFs or videos separately, it works well to combine them into a course. However you sell them, use a sales video to promote them, along with a link so customers can buy now.

As in promoting the PDF of your book, you can offer your video program by itself or with a PDF from your website. Or you can use one of the platforms, such as Clickbank, Click Funnels, or JVZoo. In addition, if your PDF is incorporated into a course, you can promote it as a course through Teachable, a website that features online courses.

Then, whatever marketing platforms you are on, you need to take additional steps to market your video programs, courses, and book or books through the traditional and/or social media.

# Teachable (www.teachable.com)

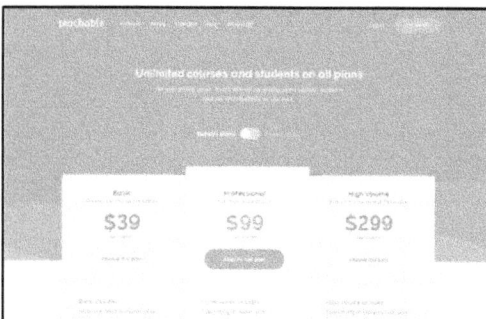

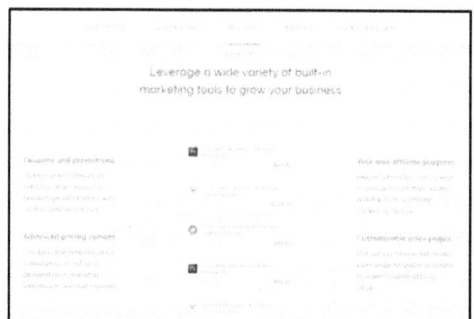

# CHAPTER 17: SETTING UP YOUR SEQUENCE FOR PUBLISHING

To determine what to do when in publishing and promoting your book, create a flow chart or spread sheet. List what you expect to do in what order, and include an approximate timeline of what you will do. Then, check off tasks as you do them. If necessary, hire one or two people to help you, and include who will do what when.

Aside from the tasks for publishing and promoting yourself or your books, include a section on the timeline which lists what you want to learn and from whom. If you plan to attend particular courses, workshops, or seminars, add them to your timeline.

Also, list your planned promotional and marketing activities, including what promotional materials you plan to develop. In this way, by listing all related tasks on the timeline, you can see the grand sweep of everything you want to do.

Feel free to change your plans as needed, and if you make changes, adapt your flow chart or spread sheet accordingly.

The flow chart is a more graphic way of presenting your plan, with arrows, lines, and circles where you write down your plans for what you are doing. If you make changes in your timing or what you expect to do, move each of these elements around, like a military commander planning how to best deploy his or her forces.

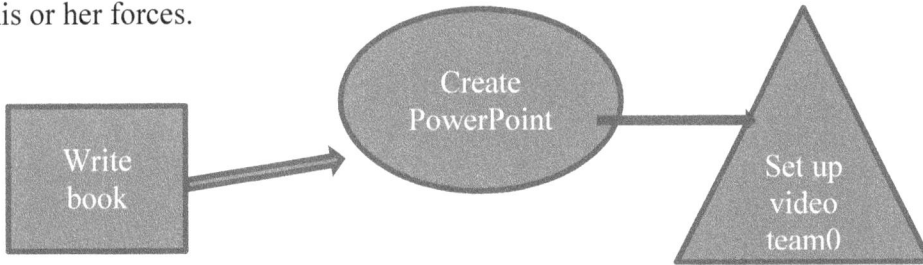

Time:
Week 1: 1/1-1/2-1/3-1/4-1/5     Week 2: 2/1-2/2-2/3-2/4-2/5     Week 3 etc.

The spreadsheet is a more linear presentation of the tasks you plan to do. The times are listed as rows and who will do them is listed in another column. To move things around, move the copy in one row to a different empty row. If there are no empty rows left for placing a task, add an additional row. You can always type in a more detailed description of the task later.

| Day-Time | Tasks by Me | Tasks by Name1 | Tasks by Name2 |
|---|---|---|---|
| 1/10 – 9:00 | | | |
| 9:15 | | | |
| 9:30 | | | |
| 9:45 | | | |
| 10:00 | | | |
| And so on for each working day | | | |
| | | | |
| | | | |
| | | | |
| | | | |
| | | | |
| | | | |
| | | | |
| | | | |

Whether you create a flow chart or spread sheet, include the approximate time you or another person need to perform these tasks, so you can easily see what you want to do and when.

# CHAPTER 18: DISTRIBUTING AND PROMOTING YOUR BOOK

Once your book is available on different publishing platforms, review the distribution arrangements provided by each platform to learn where your book will be available. These will all be non-exclusive platforms, so don't worry about any overlap. These are different ways in which people can buy your book.

You can then use this information about where your book is available in promoting your book, so you can let people know where to buy it.

For example, on your website, you might include the cover of the book, along with links on where to get it – such as in print, with a link to Amazon; in an e-book, with a link to Kindle; in an audiobook, with a link to Audible; and in a PDF, with a link to a page on your website or to a sales page on ClickBank.

## Additional Distribution Channels

Besides the basic distribution channels, such as Amazon, Kindle, Audible, and your website, consider other distribution channels, where you might sell or promote your book. Some possibilities are:
- Speaking engagements
- Workshops and seminars
- Conferences
- Trade shows and exhibits
- Book festivals
- Street and community fairs
- Competitions

In some cases, you want to be at the event personally, such as for speaking engagements, workshops, seminars, and conferences. In other cases, you may prefer to have someone representing you, such as a publicist. And some events will have their own representative who will represent your book and others, such as if you hire a book rep or company to feature your book at a trade show.

## Different Promotional Methods

Aside from doing PR through the traditional and social media, consider hiring a PR person or organization to handle your promotion. This kind of assistance can take various forms, from someone who is skilled at organizing and coordinating a publicity campaign to someone who posts or blasts out your promotional material. The basic considerations include:

- Doing your own PR
- Hiring a virtual assistant or administrative assistant to do the blasts and posts for you
- Hiring a publicist or PR service to coordinate and implement a full campaign or to set up a partial campaign where you do some of the work.

Aside from deciding on who does what work, also consider the different types of PR and what will be most effective. Some possibilities include:
- PR releases to traditional media – newspapers, magazines, Internet, radio, and TV
- Posts or ads on the major social media, which might include Facebook, Twitter, LinkedIn, and Instagram
- Short video posts, such as on Facebook Live and Periscope
- Blogs on your website
- Emails to targeted groups interested in your topic
- Emails to book reviewers and book bloggers
- Creating a sales program to make your book a #1 Amazon best-seller
- Other possibilities

If you are doing your own PR, take some time to brainstorm different approaches. Or if you are working with a professional, have a strategy session to decide what to do and who will do what.

There are many possible approaches, and you have to choose the best ones for you, based on your book's topic, the target audience, your availability for guest appearances, your budget, and other factors. Since there so many promotional possibilities and considerations, these will be considered in a future book.

# CHAPTER 19: GETTING TESTIMONIALS AND REVIEWS

As part of your PR and marketing efforts, get testimonials and reviews from book reviewers, bloggers, experts in your field, and well-known individuals interested in your subject. Then, use their endorsements in your PR efforts.

Some testimonials which you obtain before publication can go on your book cover; others can go in your promotional flyers and press releases, or on your website. Some people who like your book might contribute to your sales effort, too, especially if you have a commission or affiliate program to give them a commission on sales

Some of the sources to contact include the following:
- Friends and family members
- Business associates
- Amazon and independent book reviewers
- Book bloggers and bloggers on your topic

## Sending Out Review Copies

Ideally, send out review copies two to three months before your book is published to give reviewers, bloggers, and those who might write articles about your book plenty of time to review it in advance of publication. You can then use their reviews and testimonials as an incentive to get others to read and review your book, since the influence of peers will kick in. As more and more people review and endorse your book, more and more other people will want to do so. This way you gradually build to critical mass, where you book turns from being one of a million or more books published each year to a must read book, because so many people like it.

While it's great to get early reviews, continue seeking reviews and articles about you and your book in the weeks before and in the months after your book is out. Even late reviews 6 months or more after publication can help to kick-start more interest in your book

When you send out review copies, get as many people as possible to agree to look at copies in PDF format. Most potential endorsers and reviewers are willing to look at PDFs, and the advantage is the low cost of sending them, as well as the speed of sending and receiving them. By contrast, it costs about $3-7 for each copy of the book, depending on whether it is paperback or hardback, in color or black and white, and the number of pages. Plus, you have to add in postage and the time for packing and shipping a book, bringing the cost of about $15-20 for each book you mail out. Another disadvantage of sending hard copies is the time it takes to go to the post office or to a local packing and shipping service. Even using a shipping kiosk takes time for setting up the mailing. Then, there are several days for delivery.

So let any interested reviewers know that you hope to send a PDF, which can do immediately. If the reviewer initially requests a hard copy, let the reviewer know it will take an extra 7 to 10 days to send this out, so wouldn't he or she prefer to get a PDF quickly? In my experience, most reviewers will agree, even if they would prefer the hard copy, because it is easier for them to open the package and read a physical book – and some even have a thriving business of reselling review copies or using them as premium giveaways.

Since there are multiple strategies for finding and contacting reviewers and bloggers, this will be covered in more detail in a future book on promoting your book.

# ABOUT THE AUTHOR

GINI GRAHAM SCOTT, Ph.D., J.D., is a nationally known writer, consultant, speaker, and seminar leader, specializing in business and work relationships, professional and personal development, social trends, and popular culture. She has published over 50 books with major publishers. She has worked with dozens of clients on memoirs, self-help, popular business books, and film scripts. Writing samples are at www.ginigrahamscott.com and www.changemakerspublishingandwriting.com. She is a Huffington Post regular columnist, commenting on social trends, business, and everyday life at www.huffingtonpost.com/gini-graham-scott.

She is the founder of Changemakers Publishing, featuring books on work, business, psychology, social trends, and self-help. It has published over 50 print, e-books, and audiobooks. She has licensed several dozen books for foreign sales, including the UK, Russia, Korea, Spain, and Japan.

She has received national media exposure for her books, including appearances on *Good Morning America, Oprah,* and *CNN*. She has been the producer and host of a talk show series, *Changemakers*, featuring interviews on social trends.

Her books on business relationships and professional development include:

*Turn Your Dreams into Reality* (Llewellyn)
*Resolving Conflict* (Changemakers Publishing)
*A Survival Guide for Working with Bad Bosses* (AMACOM)
*A Survival Guide for Working with Humans* (AMACOM)
*Credit Card Fraud with Jen Grondahl Lee* (Rowman)
*Lies and Liars: How and Why Sociopaths Lie* (Skyhorse Publishing)

Scott is also active in a number of community and business groups, including the Lafayette, Pleasant Hill, and Danville Chambers of Commerce. She is a graduate of the prestigious Leadership Contra Costa program, is a7 member of two B2B groups in Danville and Walnut Creek, and a BNI member. She is the organizer of six Meetup groups in the film and publishing industries with over 5000 members in Los Angeles and the San Francisco Bay Area. She does workshops and seminars on the topics of her books.

She received her Ph.D. from the University of California, Berkeley, and her J.D. from the University of San Francisco Law School. She has received several MAs at Cal State University, East Bay.

**CHANGEMAKERS PUBLISHING**

**3527 Mt. Diablo Blvd., #273**

**Lafayette, CA 94549**

**changemakers@pacbell.net . (925) 385-0608**

**www.changemakerspublishingandwriting.com**

www.ingramcontent.com/pod-product-compliance
Lightning Source LLC
Chambersburg PA
CBHW081821200326
41597CB00023B/4336